Cryptography and Cryptanalysis in MATLAB

Creating and Programming Advanced Algorithms

Marius Iulian Mihailescu
Stefania Loredana Nita

Apress®

Cryptography and Cryptanalysis in MATLAB: Creating and Programming Advanced Algorithms

Marius Iulian Mihailescu
Bucharest, Romania

Stefania Loredana Nita
Bucharest, Romania

ISBN-13 (pbk): 978-1-4842-7333-3
https://doi.org/10.1007/978-1-4842-7334-0

ISBN-13 (electronic): 978-1-4842-7334-0

Managing Director, Apress Media LLC: Welmoed Spahr
Acquisitions Editor: Steve Anglin
Development Editor: Matthew Moodie
Editorial Operations Manager: Mark Powers

Cover designed by eStudioCalamar

Cover image by Devin Avery on Unsplash (www.unsplash.com)

Distributed to the book trade worldwide by Apress Media, LLC, 1 New York Plaza, New York, NY 10004, U.S.A. Phone 1-800-SPRINGER, fax (201) 348-4505, e-mail orders-ny@springer-sbm.com, or visit www. springeronline.com. Apress Media, LLC is a California LLC and the sole member (owner) is Springer Science + Business Media Finance Inc (SSBM Finance Inc). SSBM Finance Inc is a **Delaware** corporation.

For information on translations, please e-mail booktranslations@springernature.com; for reprint, paperback, or audio rights, please e-mail bookpermissions@springernature.com.

Apress titles may be purchased in bulk for academic, corporate, or promotional use. eBook versions and licenses are also available for most titles. For more information, reference our Print and eBook Bulk Sales web page at http://www.apress.com/bulk-sales.

Any source code or other supplementary material referenced by the author in this book is available to readers on GitHub via the book's product page, located at www.apress.com/9781484273333. For more detailed information, please visit http://www.apress.com/source-code.

Printed on acid-free paper

To our families and wonderful readers. May this book be a true inspiration for everyone…and remember: "If you think technology can solve your security problems, then you don't understand the problems and you don't understand technology." – Bruce Schneier

Table of Contents

About the Authors

Marius Iulian Mihailescu, PhD is an Associate Professor (Senior Lecturer) at the Spiru Haret University of Bucharest, Romania. He is also the CEO of Dapyx Solution Ltd., a company based in Bucharest, Romania that is focused on information security- and cryptography-related research projects. He is a lead guest editor for applied cryptography journals and a reviewer of multiple publications with information security and cryptography profiles. He has authored and co-authored more than 30 articles in conference proceedings, 25 articles in journals, and four books. For more than six years, he has served as a lecturer at well-known national and international universities (University of Bucharest, Titu Maiorescu University, Kadir Has University, Istanbul, Turkey). He has taught courses on programming languages (C#, Java, C++, and Haskell) and object-oriented system analysis and design with UML, graphs, databases, cryptography, and information security. He served for three years as an IT Officer at Royal Caribbean Cruises Ltd., where he dealt with IT infrastructure, data security, and satellite communications systems. He earned his PhD in 2014 with a thesis on applied cryptography over biometrics data. He holds two MSc degrees, in information security and software engineering.

Stefania Loredana Nita, PhD is a software developer and researcher at the Institute for Computers of the Romanian Academy. She earned her PhD with a thesis on advanced cryptographic schemes using searchable encryption and homomorphic encryption. At the Institute for Computers, she focuses on research and development projects that involve searchable encryption, homomorphic encryption, cloud computing security, the Internet of Things, and big data. She has served for more than two years as an assistant lecturer at the University of Bucharest, where she teaches advanced programming techniques, simulation methods, and operating systems. She has authored and co-authored more than 25 papers for conferences and journals and has co-authored four books. She holds an MSc in software engineering and two BSc degrees in computer science and mathematics.

About the Technical Reviewer

Irfan Turk, PhD, is a math and computer programming instructor and has worked at universities, high schools, and educational institutions for about 15 years. He concentrated on applied mathematics while earning his PhD degree. Dr. Turk finished the computer science track requirements of his MSc degree while a student at the University of Texas at Arlington. He is the author of the *Python Programming: for Engineers and Scientists* and *MATLAB Programming: for Beginners and Professionals* books. Dr. Turk's research interests include, but are not limited to, numerical solutions of differential equations, scientific computing, mathematical modeling, and programming in MATLAB and Python.

CHAPTER 1

Getting Started in Cryptography and Cryptanalysis

Due to the most recent attacks, the electronic communications and transaction require to strengthen their practical security techniques related to digital signature in such way that law enforcement agencies are able to recognize and trust them.

In the last few months alone, as we were writing this book, there were countless news stories detailing attacks that compromised the private data of millions of users on the Internet or dark web. Advanced technologies—such as the Internet of Things, fog computing, edge computing, smart vehicles, drones, smart houses, and many other complex software applications (desktop/web/mobile)—are evolving so fast that it is a challenge to keep up with their security requirements. For example, looking at the CVE platform[1], we can see a total of 152,984 records (vulnerabilities) and exposed users. By examining how these vulnerabilities occurred, developers can identify efficient ways to protect users and customers against malicious hackers.

A security solution is successful when a user's machine (computer or other electronic device) and the networks with which it communicates do not expose the data flowing between them. Because of the increasing speed and complexity of computing technology (e.g., quantum computers), the mission of modern cryptography (and we are not referring to quantum cryptography) is at a very challenging point in time.

---

[1]CVE - https://cve.mitre.org/

© Marius Iulian Mihailescu and Stefania Loredana Nita 2021
M. I. Mihailescu and S. L. Nita, *Cryptography and Cryptanalysis in MATLAB*,
https://doi.org/10.1007/978-1-4842-7334-0_1

Keeping knowledge secure is one of the most important aspects to consider when designing and implementing complex systems. Information falling into the wrong hands can result in huge financial losses or, in extreme cases, even loss of lives. Cryptography can be used to encode private information in such a way that nobody should be able to decode it without the necessary privileges. However, cryptography algorithms, have been broken after hackers found a flaw in their design. When enough computing power is applied (for example quantum computers) to break an encoded message or cryptography algorithm (such as RSA), it is only a matter of time until the encryption or algorithm will be broken.

The current work represents a continuation of previous works, such as [2] and [3], dedicated to applied cryptography using MATLAB environment for developing cryptography algorithms in a more related scientific manner. The book represents an advanced work. It provides a comprehensive view of the most important topics in information security, cryptography, and cryptanalysis. The book can be used in many areas by multiple professionals, including security experts, military experts and researchers, ethical hackers, teachers in academia, researchers, software developers, and software engineers. If you need security and cryptographic solutions in a real business software environment, this book represents a very good starting point, together with [1] and [2]. The book will serve very useful for students (undergraduate- and graduate-level, master degree, professional, and academic doctoral degree students), business analysts, and many others.

Cryptography and Cryptanalysis

There are three main concepts to keep in mind when dealing with information security and data protection. Those concepts are *cryptology, cryptography,* and *cryptanalysis.*

- *"Cryptology* is defined as the science or art of secret writings; the main goal is to protect and defend the secrecy and confidentiality of the information with the help of cryptographic algorithms." [2, 3].

- *"Cryptography* represents the defensive side of the cryptology; the main objective is to create and design the cryptographic systems and their rules. When we are dealing with cryptography, we can observe a special kind of art; an art that is based on protecting the information by transforming it into an unreadable format, called ciphertext." [2, 3].

- *"Cryptanalysis* is the offensive side of the cryptology; its main objective is to study the cryptographic systems with the scope to provide the necessary characteristics in such a way as to fulfill the function for which they have been designed. Cryptanalysis can analyze the cryptographic systems of third parties through the cryptograms realized with them, in such a way that breaks them to obtain useful information for their business purposes. Cryptanalysts, code breakers, or ethical hackers are the people who are dealing with the field of cryptanalysis." [2, 3].

- *"Cryptographic primitive* represents a well-established or low-level cryptographic algorithm used to build cryptographic protocols. Examples of such routines include hash functions and encryption functions." [2, 3].

The book provides a deep examination of all three concepts from the practical side to the theoretical side. It illustrates how a theoretical algorithm should be analyzed for implementation.

Book Structure

The book is divided into 14 chapters meant to cover the most important practical and theoretical aspects of modern cryptography and cryptanalysis. The chapters are structured in such a manner that they cover the key elements, from theoretical cryptography to applied cryptography, especially when implementing the algorithms in MATLAB.

Each chapter is structured into two main parts—the *mathematical background,* which provides the notions required in the implementation process, and the *implementation,* which contains examples of how it should be done. The chapter goals are as follows:

- *Chapter 1.* This chapter's goal is to highlight the importance of cryptography and cryptanalysis, justifying the importance of applied cryptography in a continuously evolving period of technology and requirements.

- *Chapter 2*. This chapter gives a short introduction to the built-in functions from MATLAB that are used to implement the cryptographic algorithms.

- *Chapter 3*. This chapter explains the different procedures for converting text (messages/plaintext) from lowercase to uppercase, from ASCII codes to characters, etc. These conversions are very useful in cryptography for some special algorithms.

- *Chapter 4*. This chapter covers the main arithmetic operations that are dedicated to cryptography algorithms. Every arithmetic operation is justified through an example, with the goal to make it clear as it how it should be done correctly in MATALB.

- *Chapter 5*. In cryptography, especially in theoretical cryptography, number theory represents an important part of the research when designing and proposing new cryptography algorithms. Number theory is a fascinating and complex field. Without a proper understanding of its theoretical concepts, developers cannot perform a correct and reliable implementation of a cryptography algorithm. The purpose of this chapter is to give important highlights of important aspects that are useful to those who want to write cryptography algorithms from scratch.

- *Chapter 6*. This chapter contains the implementation of well-known algorithms (e.g., Caesar, Vigenère, and Hill) in order to provide the readers with a strong foundation of the main operations from MATLAB that are used to implement the cryptography algorithms. Each algorithm is done with respect to the two main operations, encryption and decryption.

- *Chapter 7*. This chapter covers the most important aspects of generating random numbers. This chapter is dedicated to those cryptography algorithms in which generating high random numbers is an important part of the security of the cryptography algorithm.

- *Chapter 8*. This chapter presents an implementation of hash functions, such as MD4/MD5, SHA1/256/368/512. It explores the fascinating processes behind generating hashes for different types of data, such as text.

- *Chapter 9.* This chapter presents the main implementation procedure based on the proposed standards by NIST for DES (Data Encryption Standard) and AES (Advanced Encryption System). Designing s-boxes is an important concept in DES and AES [1]. The chapter will examine the construction of S-boxes and underline their importance in implementing cryptographic algorithms.

- *Chapter 10.* This chapter is dedicated to one of the most important types of cryptography, AES. This chapter presents advanced notions and concepts for public-key cryptography that are very useful in designing and implementing advanced, complex systems.

- *Chapter 11.* This chapter goes through a series of advanced, powerful algorithms, such as RSA and ElGamal. They are used every day in many applications (e.g., Internet browsers).

- *Chapter 12.* This chapter provides techniques for allowing visual information, such as pictures, to be encrypted in such way that the decrypted information is shown as a visual image.

- *Chapter 13.* This chapter represents encryption and decryption methods using chaos theory and chaos algorithms proposed at the theoretical level. Chaos-based cryptography is a controversial topic due to the complexity of the operations and the field itself.

- *Chapter 14.* This chapter provides different implementations of methods and algorithms for *steganography*, which is the art of hiding different types of data (text and files) in another type of media file (pictures files, text files, etc.).

Conclusion

In this first chapter, we discussed the objectives of this book, based on addressing the practical aspects of cryptography and information security. Due to the increasing number of requirements for developing secure software applications and using advanced information technologies, they have a deep impact on our lives every day.

The goal of this book is translate the most important theoretical cryptography algorithms and mechanism to practice using one of the most powerful technologies in research, MATLAB.

In this chapter you learned about:

- The mission and goals of this book.

- The differences between cryptography, cryptanalysis, and cryptology.

- The goal of each chapter and the algorithms presented.

References

[1]   *Modern Cryptography Applied Mathematics for Encryption and Information Security,* William Easttom, Springer, 2021.

[2]   Mihailescu, Marius Iulian, and Stefania Loredana Nita. *Pro Cryptography and Cryptanalysis: Creating Advanced Algorithms with C# and .NET.* Apress, 2021. DOI: 10.1007/978-1-4842-6367-9.

[3]   Mihailescu, Marius Iulian, and Stefania Loredana Nita. *Pro Cryptography and Cryptanalysis with C++20: Creating and Programming Advanced Algorithms.* Apress, 2021. DOI: 10.1007/978-1-4842-6586-4.

CHAPTER 2

MATLAB Cryptography Functions

One of the most important elements in cryptography is the *bit*, the foundation of digital information. Working with bits requires different logical operations, such as OR, AND, or XOR. MATLAB implements these operators automatically, as well as some types of conversions to bits, as you will see in this chapter. Other important aspects of cryptography are *arrays* or *matrices*. These have many applications. For example, the elements of a finite group are stored in an array, and the key of an encryption system uses matrices to be generated. In this chapter, you will see some of the most important functions that work with bits and matrices.

In MATLAB, there are several functions already implemented that work directly with bits to implement the main operations on bits (*bitwise* operations). Examples of such functions are `bitset`, `bitget`, `bitshift`, `bitcmp`, `bitor`, `bitand`, `bitxor`, and `swapbytes` [1]. They all take numeric values as input. These functions are defined as follows:

- `Bitset`: Sets a bit value on a given location.

- `Bitget`: Gets the bit value from a given location.

- `Bitshift`: Shifts the bits with a specific number of locations. The sense of shifting (left or right) and the bits that fill the initial places are given by the signs of the bits that need to be shifted and the number of locations to be shifted.

- `Bitcmp`: Returns the complement of the bit(s) given as input.

- `Bitor`: Returns the result of the OR operation between the bits.

- `Bitand`: Returns the result of the AND operation between the bits.

© Marius Iulian Mihailescu and Stefania Loredana Nita 2021
M. I. Mihailescu and S. L. Nita, *Cryptography and Cryptanalysis in MATLAB*,
https://doi.org/10.1007/978-1-4842-7334-0_2

- Bitxor: Returns the result of the XOR operation between the bits.

- Swapbytes: Swaps of the order of the bytes.

Listing 2-1 presents the applications of these functions; the result is shown in Figure 2-1.

Listing 2-1. Using a Bitwise Function from MATLAB

```
1
2   clc;
3   clear all;
4
5   no1 = 25;
6   bin1 = dec2bin(no1);
7   fprintf("The binary value of %d is: %s. \n", no1, bin1);
8   no2 = -65;
9   bin1 = dec2bin(no2);
10  fprintf("The binary value of %d is: %s. \n", no2, bin1);
11  fprintf("\n");
12
13  no3 = 1739;
14  set_res = bitset(no3, 5);
15  fprintf("Changing the second bit of %d to 1 results in: %d. \n", no3,
16  set_res);
17  fprintf("\n");
18
19  get_res = bitget(no3,3);
20  fprintf("The binary value of %d is %s and the 3rd bit is %d. \n", no3,
21  dec2bin(no1), get_res);
22  fprintf("\n");
23
24  no4 = round(2000 +(10000-2000)*rand(1,1));
25  shift_res = bitshift(no4, 5);
26  fprintf("Shifting 5 bits to left of %d (%s) results in %d (%s). \n",
27  no4, dec2bin(no4), shift_res, dec2bin(shift_res));
28  shift_res2 = bitshift(no4, -5);
```

```matlab
29    fprintf("Shifting 5 bits to right of %d (%s) results in %d (%s). \n",
30    no4, dec2bin(no4), shift_res2, dec2bin(shift_res2));
31    shift_res = bitshift(0-no4, 5, 'int64');
32    fprintf("Shifting 5 bits to left of %d (%s) results in %d (%s). \n",
33    no4, dec2bin(no4), shift_res, dec2bin(shift_res));
34    shift_res2 = bitshift(0-no4, -5, 'int64');
35    fprintf("Shifting 5 bits to right of %d (%s) results in %d (%s). \n",
36    no4, dec2bin(no4), shift_res2, dec2bin(shift_res2));
37    fprintf("\n");
38
39    cmp_res = bitcmp(no4, 'int64');
40    fprintf("The bit-wise complement of %d (%s) is %d (%s). \n", no4,
41    dec2bin(no4), cmp_res, dec2bin(cmp_res));
42    fprintf("\n");
43
44    no5 = round(2000 +(10000-2000)*rand(1,1));
45    fprintf("%d (%s) OR %d (%s) = %d (%s) \n", no4, dec2bin(no4), no5,
46    dec2bin(no5), bitor(no4,no5), dec2bin(bitor(no4,no5)));
47    fprintf("%d (%s) AND %d (%s) = %d (%s) \n", no4, dec2bin(no4), no5,
48    dec2bin(no5), bitand(no4,no5), dec2bin(bitand(no4,no5)));
49    fprintf("%d (%s) XOR %d (%s) = %d (%s) \n", no4, dec2bin(no4), no5,
      dec2bin(no5), bitxor(no4,no5), dec2bin(bitxor(no4,no5)));
50    fprintf("\n");
51
52    no6 = 0x134DF5ED;
53    swap_res = swapbytes(no6);
      fprintf("Number  %d (%s) swapped is %d (%s). \n", no6, dec2hex(no6),
      swap_res, dec2hex(swap_res));
```

```
Command Window                                                                    —   □   ×

The binary value of 25 is: 11001.
The binary value of -65 is: 10111111.

Changing the second bit of 1739 to 1 results in: 1755.

The binary value of 1739 is 11001 and the 3rd bit is 0.

Shifting 5 bits to left of 9602 (10010110000010) results in 307264 (1001011000001000000).
Shifting 5 bits to right of 9602 (10010110000010) results in 300 (100101100).
Shifting 5 bits to left of 9602 (10010110000010) results in -307264 (111111111111101101001111111000000).
Shifting 5 bits to right of 9602 (10010110000010) results in -301 (1111111011010011).

The bit-wise complement of 9602 (10010110000010) is -9603 (1101101001111101).

9602 (10010110000010) OR 2276 (100011100100) = 11750 (10110111100110)
9602 (10010110000010) AND 2276 (100011100100) = 128 (10000000)
9602 (10010110000010) XOR 2276 (100011100100) = 11622 (10110101100110)

Number  323876333 (134DF5ED) swapped is 3992276243 (EDF54D13).
fx >> |
```

Figure 2-1. *The results obtained using bitwise functions*

We started with the `clc;` and `clear all;` commands, which are used to clear the Command Window, in order to remove all items from the workspace and release the corresponding occupied memory. MATLAB provides different types of conversion functions. One of these functions is `dec2bin`, which converts a decimal number into its corresponding binary representation. Another example of a conversion function is `dec2hex`, which converts a decimal number into its hexadecimal representation. A complete list of conversion functions can be found at [2].

Note that the code in Listing 2-1 uses the `rand` function for `no4` and `no5`, so every time the program runs, different results will be obtained. This function, without parameters, generates a random number in the $(0, 1)$ interval. However, Listing 2-1 uses `rand(1,1)`, which generates a 1×1 matrix, which actually means one element. In general, `rand(a,b)` generates a $a \times b$ matrix, with elements in the $(0, 1)$ interval. Note also that `no4` and `no5` are not in the interval $(0, 1)$ and we used a formula to generate them. The general formula is

$$x + (y - x) * rand(1,1)$$

to generate a number in the interval (x, y). As we used $x = 2000$ and $y = 10000$, `no4` and `no5` were generated in this interval. The values for `no4` and `no5` are integer values because we used the `round` function to round the result.

Next, we provide some examples that involve matrices and arrays. These are very useful in different kinds of cryptography applications, for example, to generate keys or to test different properties of the key, such as its length. Listing 2-2 presents some examples implemented in MATLAB.

Listing 2-2. Working with Matrices

```
1
2    clc;
3    clear all;
4
5    fprintf("Generating matrix... \n");
6    min_lim = 100;
7    max_lim = 1000;
8    v = round(min_lim +(max_lim-
9    min_lim)*rand(2,10));
10   disp(v);
11
12   fprintf("The length of v is %d. \n",
13   length(v));
14   fprintf("The size of v is %d. \n",
15   size(v));
16
17   fprintf("v has %d elements. \n", numel(v));
18   fprintf("\n");
19   fprintf("Sorting v... \n");
20   disp(sort(v));
21
22   fprintf("Sorting rows of v... \n");
23   disp(sortrows(v));
24
25   fprintf("Flipping v... \n");
26   disp(flip(v));
27
28   fprintf("Reshaping v... \n");
29   v2 = reshape(v, [5,4]);
```

```
30    disp(v2);
      fprintf("Replicating v...\n");
      v3 = repmat(v,2);
      disp(v3);
```

The result of Listing 2-2 is presented in Figure 2-2.

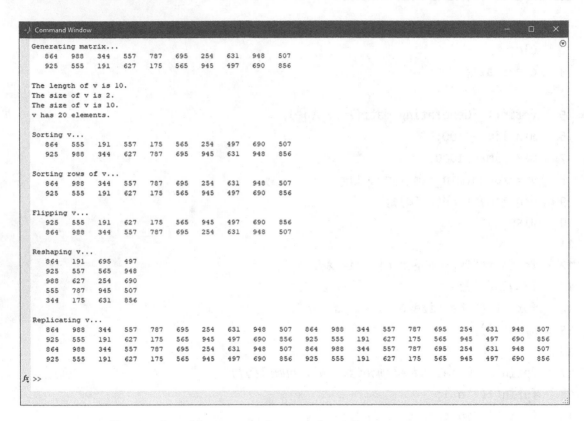

Figure 2-2. *The results of functions that work with matrices*

In line 7 of Listing 2-2, we generated a matrix with 2 rows and 10 columns, with random integer numbers in the [100, 1000] interval. In line 10, we printed the length of the matrix. The length is given by the longest sub-array in an array. As a matrix can be seen as an array of arrays, the result of this example is 10, because each line contains 10 elements. Therefore, the size of the matrix is 10. If v would have been composed of sub-arrays with different lengths, the length of v would have been equal to the number of elements of the longest sub-array. Next, the size of the matrix gives the number of rows and columns, while the numel function gives the total number of elements in the matrix. The sort function sorts the elements of each column of the matrix, while sortrows sorts the elements of each row of the matrix. The `flip` function flips the elements between the columns of the matrix. Next, `reshape` generates another matrix with a total number of elements that's the same as the original matrix, but with a different number of rows and columns. Finally, `repmat` replicates the matrix by the given number of times, in our example, two times. Note that all these functions can be applied on arrays too.

The following functions are representative of different operations in cryptography, including functions such as `eig` (see Figure 2-3), `poly` (see Figure 2-4), and `roots` (see Figure 2-5).

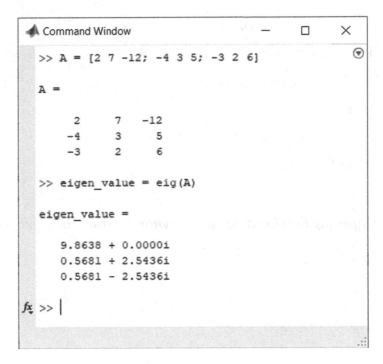

Figure 2-3. *Computing eigen values using the eig function*

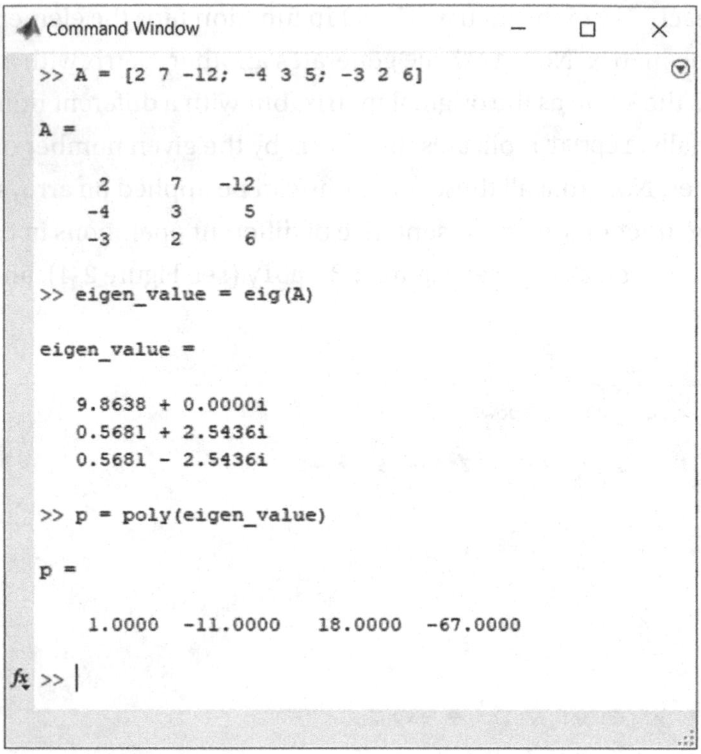

```
Command Window                                    —    □    ×
>> A = [2 7 -12; -4 3 5; -3 2 6]

A =

    2    7   -12
   -4    3    5
   -3    2    6

>> eigen_value = eig(A)

eigen_value =

   9.8638 + 0.0000i
   0.5681 + 2.5436i
   0.5681 - 2.5436i

>> p = poly(eigen_value)

p =

    1.0000  -11.0000   18.0000   -67.0000

fx >> |
```

Figure 2-4. *Computing the characteristic polynomial from the eigen_value values*

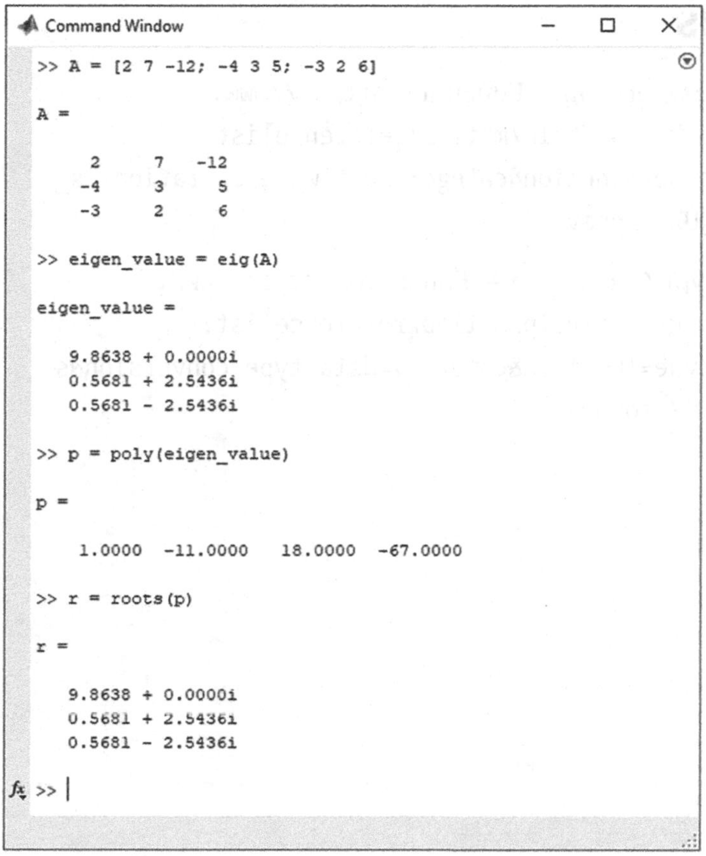

```
Command Window                                    —    □    ×
>> A = [2 7 -12; -4 3 5; -3 2 6]

A =

     2     7    -12
    -4     3     5
    -3     2     6

>> eigen_value = eig(A)

eigen_value =

   9.8638 + 0.0000i
   0.5681 + 2.5436i
   0.5681 - 2.5436i

>> p = poly(eigen_value)

p =

    1.0000   -11.0000    18.0000   -67.0000

>> r = roots(p)

r =

   9.8638 + 0.0000i
   0.5681 + 2.5436i
   0.5681 - 2.5436i

fx >> |
```

Figure 2-5. *Computing the roots using the roots function*

Conclusion

This chapter presented the main functions that work directly on bits and explained how to work with characteristics of matrices and arrays. These functions, matrices, and arrays are very useful in implementing cryptographic algorithms.

References

[1]   Bitwise Operations – Functions: `https://www.mathworks.com/help/matlab/referencelist.html?type=function&category=bit-wise-operations&s_tid=CRUX_topnav`

[2]   Data Type Conversion — Functions: `https://www.mathworks.com/help/matlab/referencelist.html?type=function&category=data-type-conversion&s_tid=CRUX_topnav`

CHAPTER 3

Conversions Used in MATLAB for Cryptography

The goal of this chapter is to provide a quick overview of the main conversion mechanisms for numbers and strings that are specific to the cryptography field. Representing numbers and binary strings in different bases is one of the most critical steps in cryptography. This chapter covers the main steps and discusses how they are done properly in MATLAB.

A common example used in cryptographic operations is the process of converting integers into lowercase and uppercase strings. Listing 3-1 and Figure 3-1 show an example of converting integers into lowercase strings.

In Line 1 of Listing 3-1, we define the signature of the function. The call of the function receives an integer array with a length between 0 and 25 (see Line 2). If the size is not between those values, an error is thrown, informing the user about the size that should be provided (see Line 3). Line 6 shows the conversion process provided by the char function, which is a built-in MATLAB function.

Listing 3-1. Converting Integers Into Lowercase Strings

```
1   function converted_output_string = Listing3_1(integer_array)
2   while  (max((integer_array < 0) | (integer_array > 25))) > 0
3       error('The integer value provided has to be situated between 0
        and 25.');
4   end
5
6   converted_output_string = char(integer_array + 'a');
```

© Marius Iulian Mihailescu and Stefania Loredana Nita 2021
M. I. Mihailescu and S. L. Nita, *Cryptography and Cryptanalysis in MATLAB*,
https://doi.org/10.1007/978-1-4842-7334-0_3

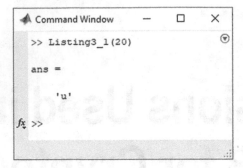

Figure 3-1. *Result of converting an integer into a lowercase string*

In Listing 3-2 and Figure 3-2 we have a similar example; the difference is that the integers are converted into uppercase letters.

Listing 3-2. Converting Integers Into Uppercase Strings

```
1    function converted_output_string = Listing3_2(integer_array)
2
3    while (max((integer_array < 0) | (integer_array > 25))) > 0
4        error('The integer value provided has to be situated between 0
         and 25.');
5    end
6
7    converted_output_string = char(integer_array + 'A');
```

Figure 3-2. *Result of converting an integer into an uppercase string*

Listing 3-3 and Figure 3-3 show another example. This time the process is reversed—the program converts from letters to integers. The process is similar and the signature of the function is declared in the same way as in the examples in Listings 3-1 and 3-2.

In Line 3 of Listing 3-3, there is the condition that the string array characters must be situated between *a* and *z*. If another character is encountered within the string, an error message is thrown (see Line 4). In Line 7, the conversion is performed and returned to the user.

Listing 3-3. Converting Lowercase Strings Into Integers

```
1   function output_array = Listing3_3(string_array)
2
3   while (max((string_array < 'a') + (string_array > 'z'))) > 0
4       error('Integer value provided has to be lower-case letter.');
5   end
6
7   output_array = string_array - 'a';
```

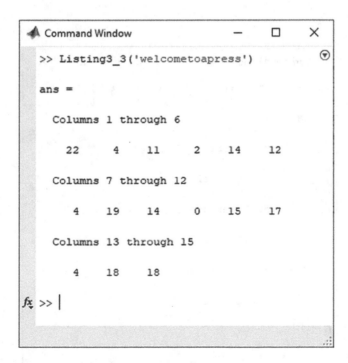

Figure 3-3. *Output of integer conversion to uppercase strings*

In Listing 3-4 and Figure 3-4, we have another example of converting a lowercase string (including the spaces between words) to an array of integers. In Line 1, we have the signature of the function; the parameter is represented by the string that the user will enter (see Figure 3-4). In Line 3, we loop through each character of the string and run the tests provided for each character, then convert them properly (see Lines 4, 5, and 7).

Listing 3-4. Converting a Lowercase String That Contains Spaces to an Array of Integers

```
1    function output_array = Listing3_4(string_array)
2
3    for i=1:length(string_array)
4       if  double(string_array(i)) > 32
5           output_array(i) = double(string_array(i))-97;
6       else
7           output_array(i) = 26;
8       end
9    end
```

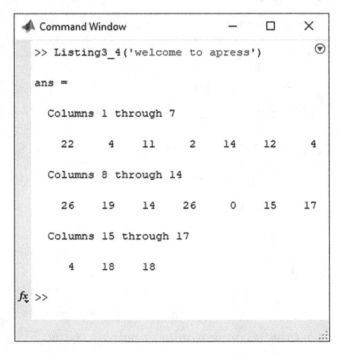

Figure 3-4. *Output of converting a lowercase string with spaces to an array of integers*

The example in Listing 3-5 is an implementation of converting a string with uppercase letters to an integer array (see Figure 3-5 for the output). The implementation is similar to the implementations provided in Listings 3-1 and 3-2.

Listing 3-5. Converting an Uppercase String to an Integer Array

```
1   function output_array = Listing3_5(string_array)
2
3   while (max((string_array < 'A') + (string_array > 'Z'))) > 0
4       error('The text provided must be only capital letters');
5   end
6
7   output_array = string_array - 'A';
```

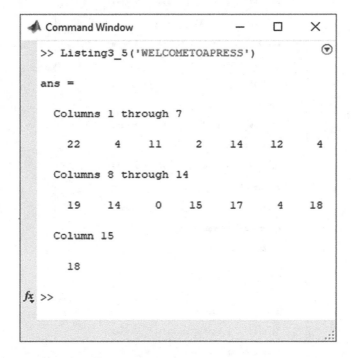

Figure 3-5. *Output of converting an uppercase string to an integer array*

The example in Listing 3-6 generates random numbers. This example can be used to implement pseudo-random number generators. The implementation provided in Listing 3-6 is quite straightforward and simple to follow. The signature of the function receives three parameters—the minimum and maximum values represent the number of digits, and the length determines how long the random number will be (see Figure 3-6).

21

Listing 3-6. Generating Random Numbers

```
1    function array_output = Listing3_6(minimum, maximum, length)
2    f = floor(maximum +1- minimum);
3    r = rand(1,length);
4    array_output = minimum + (f * r);
```

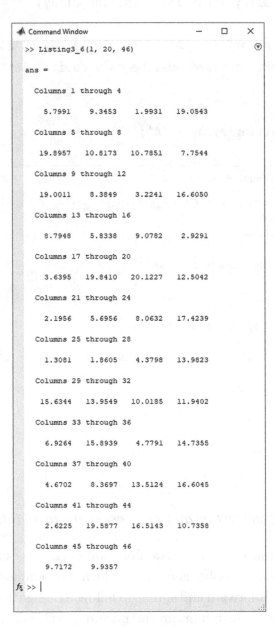

Figure 3-6. *Output of generating random numbers*

Conclusion

This chapter discussed several basic examples that illustrate different conversion scenarios. These examples are very useful for implementing cryptographic algorithms. They are one of the simplest and most reliable ways of implementing such conversion methods.

References

[1]   Turk, Irfan. *Practical MATLAB: With Modeling, Simulation, and Processing Projects.* Apress, 2019. DOI.org (Crossref), doi:10.1007/978-1-4842-5281-9.

[2]   Eshkabilov, Sulaymon. *Beginning MATLAB and Simulink: From Novice to Professional.* 2019. Open WorldCat, `https://search.ebscohost.com/login.aspx?direct=true&scope=site&db=nlebk&db=nlabk&AN=2320660`.

[3]   Hunt, Brian R., et al. A Guide to MATLAB: For Beginners and Experienced Users. Cambridge University Press, 2001.

[4]   Gander, Walter. *Learning MATLAB*. Springer International Publishing, 2015. *DOI.org (Crossref)*, doi:10.1007/978-3-319-25327-5.

[5]   Gustafsson, Fredrik, and Niclas Bergman. *MATLAB for Engineers Explained*. Springer London, 2003. *DOI.org (Crossref)*, doi:10.1007/978-1-4471-0029-4.

CHAPTER 4

Basic Arithmetic Foundations

In cryptography, the Integer Factorization Problem (IFP) has significant importance because many cryptosystems with public keys ground their security on the hardness assumption of it. For example, RSA Laboratories launched many competitions that targeted IFPs [1]. The IFP problem consists of writing an arbitrary integer as a product of powers of prime numbers. Note that every integer number can be written as a product of prime numbers and that product is unique. At the same time, IFP is interesting because it combines elements of number theory with elements of complexity theory.

However, to factorize an integer number, it is enough to find an algorithm that defines the given integer as a product of two integers (greater than one). This problem is known as *splitting* and if such an algorithm existed, it would be applied recursively until the complete factorization of any integer is found. This is of interest for odd integers only, because factoring an even integer leads to dividing by two until an odd integer is obtained, which is then split on its turn.

The purpose of this chapter is to provide a quick overview of the main tools used to deal with numbers and their basic operations in cryptography.

Another important tool in cryptography are *big integers*, which are numbers with hundreds or thousands of digits. For these, the IFP becomes interesting, because there are no efficient solutions, except for the following situations [2]:

- $n = p$. The integer n is actually a prime number. For this, primality tests can be applied, which are much more efficient than factorization algorithms.

© Marius Iulian Mihailescu and Stefania Loredana Nita 2021
M. I. Mihailescu and S. L. Nita, *Cryptography and Cryptanalysis in MATLAB*,
https://doi.org/10.1007/978-1-4842-7334-0_4

- $n = p^a$. The integer n is a power of a prime number p, so it can be extracted recursively by the root of order i. It verifies that the root of order i is an integer number. The time complexity of this algorithm is logarithmic (a binary search can be used).

- *Special integers.* The integer contains factors that have properties that enable efficient use.

The factorization problem is approached differently depending on the case used. In cryptography, the case whereby $n = p \cdot q$, where p and q are prime numbers, is very important. There are two main categories for factorization algorithms:

- *Dedicated algorithms* (applied for special cases of integers): These algorithms are used to compute factors smaller than a given threshold, which, in practice, is established based on computational resources. Examples of such algorithms are Exhaustive Search, the Euclidean algorithm, the Fermat algorithm, the Pollard p-1 algorithm, the Pollard Rho algorithm, Elliptic Curves, etc.

- *General algorithms*: These algorithms are used to factorize integers with large factors. Examples of such algorithms are Quadratic Sieve Factoring, the Number Field Sieve, etc.

The Exhaustive Search, which is the most inefficient algorithm, divides n into successive integer values in the interval $\left[2, \sqrt{n} \right]$ with the purpose of finding a factor. The complexity for the Exhaustive Search is $O\left(\sqrt{n} \right)$, which is unpractical for big integers with hundreds or thousands of bits.

This chapter presents the Euclid algorithm and the Extended Euclidean algorithm. First, let's establish some guidelines. Note that we briefly present the main ideas that will be used in this chapter, similarly with [2] and [6]. A comprehensive source about the number theory used in cryptography is [2]. [3]-[5] are also good references.

Euclid's Division Lemma

Let $a \in \mathbb{N}^*$, $b \in \mathbb{Z}$. Then unique $q, r \in \mathbb{Z}$ exist with the following properties:

(a) $a = b \cdot q + r$

(b) $0 \leq r < b$

We say "*b* divides *a*" (denoted *b* | *a*) or "*a* is multiple of *b*" or "*b* is a divisor of *a*" when the remainder of the division of *a* into *b* is zero ($r = 0$). For two numbers $m, n \in \mathbb{Z}$, a *common divisor* is a natural number *d* that divides *m* and *n* simultaneously.

Greatest Common Divisor (gcd)

Let a, b $\in \mathbb{Z}^*$. The gcd between two integers *a* and *b* is the unique number $g \in \mathbb{N}$ with the following properties:

(a) $g \mid a$ and $g \mid b$

(b) *For any* $c \in \mathbb{N}$: *if* $c \mid a$ *and* $c \mid b$, *then* $c \mid g$

The notation for *g* is $g = gcd\,(a, b)$, or simply, $g = (a, b)$. If $(a, b) = 1$, then *a* and *b* are called *coprime numbers*. Note that coprime numbers are also called *relatively* prime numbers.

A notion related to the *gcd* is the *least common multiple* between to integer numbers *a* and *b*. It is denoted as *lcm*(*a*, *b*), or simply [*a*, *b*] and represents the least natural number that is divisible with *a* and *b*.

Euclid's Algorithm

Let a, b $\in \mathbb{Z}$, a $\geq$ b > 0 and the initialization notation a = r_{-1}, b = r_0. By applying Euclid's division lemma repeatedly, this will be achieved

$$r_{j-1} = r_j \cdot q_{j+1} + r_{j+1}, 0 < r_{j+1} < r_j$$

for all values 0 $\leq$ j < n, where *n* is the first prime number with the property $r_{n+1} = 0$. Then (a, b) = r_n.

The factorization based on Euclid's algorithm supposes to construct the product $P_k = \prod_{i=1}^{k} p_i$ of the first *k* prime numbers and then compute gcd(*n*, P_k), where *n* is the numbers that should be factorized. This solution is not more efficient than the Exhaustive Search, and also requires memory space for storing the products—space that is not available when working with big integers. However, Euclid's algorithm has an advantage that allows it to be used in practice. Tables with products of the above form can be computed for reasonable values apriori knowing the number *n*, which can be used to compute the small factors of any integer that is desired to be factored.

The Extended Euclidean Algorithm

Let a, b $\in \mathbb{N}$ and q_i, $1 \leq i \leq n + 1$ be the quotients obtained by applying Euclid's Algorithm for computing g = (a, b) (n is the first positive index with $r_{n+1} = 0$). If $s_1 = 1$ and $s_0 = 0$ and

$$s_i = s_{i-2} - q_{n-i+2} \cdot s_{i-1}, 1 \leq i \leq n+1,$$

then g = s_{n+1}a + s_nb.

Another important topic used in cryptography is the congruence in the ring $(\mathbb{Z}_n, +, \cdot)$, where $\mathbb{Z}_n = \{0, \ldots, n - 1\}$. Let $a, b \in \mathbb{Z}$, $n \in \mathbb{N}^*$; a is congruent with b modulo n if n divides $(a - b)$, and it is denoted $a \equiv b \, (mod \, n)$. Recall that all number theory used in cryptography is explained in detail in [2]; of interest here is how the modular inverse is computed.

Let $a \in \mathbb{Z}$, $n \in \mathbb{N}^*$. The multiplicative (or modular) inverse of $a \, (modulo \, n)$ is the positive integer $x < n$ with $ax \equiv 1 (mod \, n)$ and it is denoted $x = a^{-1}$. The inverse of a number in $\mathbb{Z}_n$ can be computed using the Extended Euclidean algorithm. Considering n prime and $b \in \mathbb{Z}_n$, the Extended Euclidean algorithm is applied for the pair (b, n) and it is found in the value $g = s_{p+1}b + s_p n$, where p is the first positive index with $r_{p+1} = 0$. But $g = 1$, because n is prime, and if this relation is taken as a congruence modulo n, then it is achieved $1 \equiv s_{p+1} \cdot b \, (mod \, n)$. Therefore, $s_{p+1} = b^{-1}(mod \, n)$.

Practical Implementations

This section covers the importance of arithmetic foundations in cryptography. We point out some of the most useful algorithms, such as the Extended Euclidean algorithm and Exhaustive Search.

The Extended Euclidean Algorithm

In Listing 4-1 and Figure 4-1, we can see an implementation of the Extended Euclidean algorithm, which is one of the most basic and simplest algorithms used in cryptography. In Lines 2 and 3, we are reading two numbers from the user as input. In Lines 5 and 17, we are validating the data entered by the user. In Line 20, the remainder is computed by following the theoretical notions presented previously. Between Lines 23 and 27, we are computing the remainder if it is different from zero. In Line 30, we are showing the output (see Figure 4-1). Of course, for the implementation in Listing 4-1, MATLAB offers the function $GCD(a,b)$, which does the same thing. The purpose here is to understand the main mechanisms behind the functions and to provide a starting point for readers, with the goal of developing personal functions or improving them for their projects.

Listing 4-1. The Extended Euclidean Algorithm

```
1    % positive numbers should be entered by the user
2    x = input('Enter number X = ');
3    y = input('Enter number Y = ');
4
5    % validation of X number
6    if isempty(x)
7        error 'Number X -> You need to enter a value. Non-empty values are
         not allowed';
8    else
9        x = abs(x);
10   end
11
12   % validation of Y number
13   if isempty(y)
14       error 'Number Y -> You need to enter a value. Non-empty values are
         not allowed';
15   else
16       y = abs(y);
17   end
18
19   % computing the remainder
20   remainder = x - y*floor(x/y);
21
22   % we will perform untill
23   while remainder ~= 0
24       x = y;
25       y = remainder ;
26       remainder = x - y*floor(x/y);
27   end
28
29   % show the result
30   GreatCommonDivisor = y
```

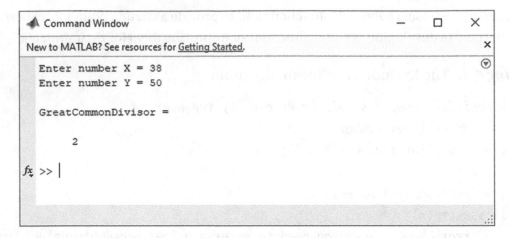

Figure 4-1. *Output of the Extended Euclidian algorithm from Listing 4-1*

Prime Factors in MATLAB

Working in cryptography with prime factors is the core of many cryptographic algorithms. Comparing other programming languages (e.g., C++, Java, Python, C#, etc.) with MATLAB, computing prime factors is a very easy task. This section provides a few examples of how to use the `factor` function from MATLAB.

The `factor` function has the *prime_ factor = factor(n)* syntax, according to [7]. The purpose of this function is to return a row array in which its elements are the prime factors of *n*. The *prime_ factor* array has the same data type as *n*.

In order to compute the prime factors, it is enough to invoke the following command in the Command Window (see Figure 4-2):

prime_ factor=factor(500)

If, for example, we need to compute the product of the prime factors from the *prime_ factor* array, we can use the `prod(prime_factor)` function. See Figure 4-3 for the output.

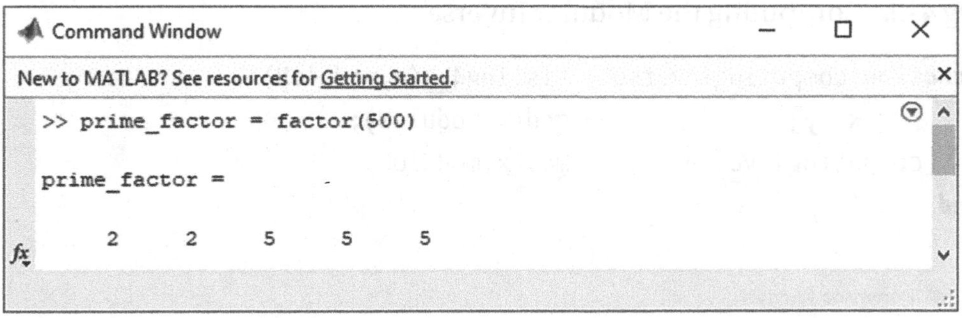

Figure 4-2. *Computing prime factors using the factor function*

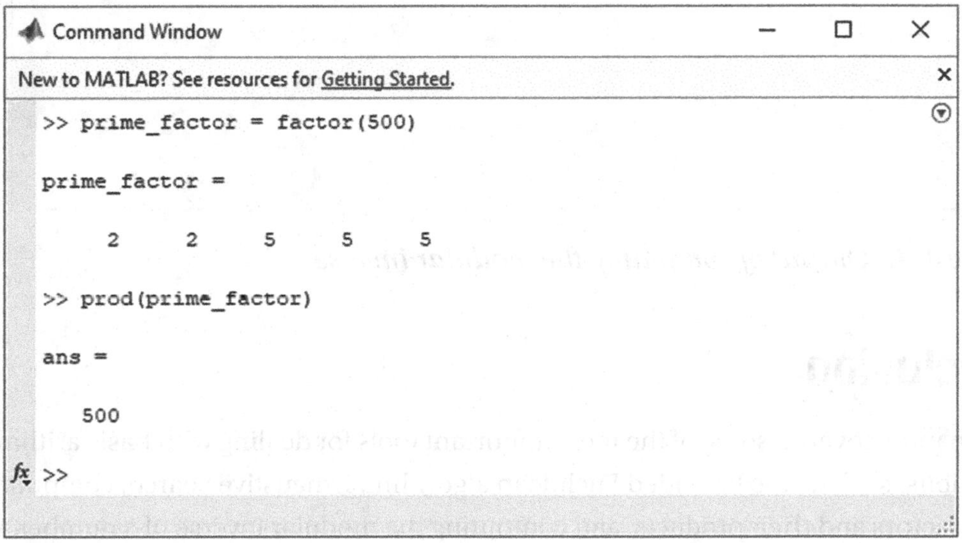

Figure 4-3. *Computing the product of prime factors*

Computing the Modular Inverse

In Listing 4-2, we provide a very simple implementation on how to compute the modulo inverse of a number. It is quite straightforward and simple to use. See Figure 4-4 for the output. In Line 2, the gcd function can be replaced with the function that we provided in Listing 4-1. In Line 3, the MATLAB built-in function mod is used to compute the inverse of x.

Listing 4-2. Computing the Modular Inverse

```
1   function computingInverse = Listing4_3(w,moduloN)
2       [d, x, y]              = gcd(w,moduloN);
3       computingInverse      = mod(x,moduloN);
4   end
```

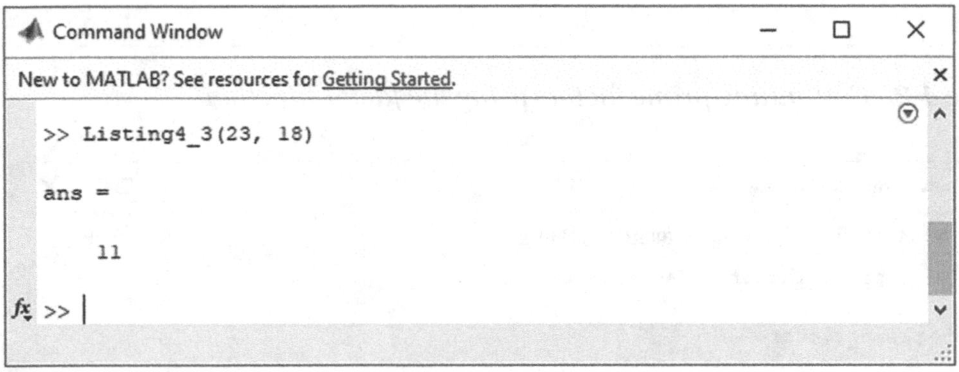

Figure 4-4. *Output of computing the modular inverse*

Conclusion

This chapter covered some of the most important tools for dealing with basic arithmetic operations, such as the Extended Euclidean algorithm, Exhaustive Search, computing prime factors and their products, and computing the modular inverse of a number. We provide the main theoretical concepts as a starting point in the field of number theory. The set of references can be used to complete your knowledge about number theory.

References

[1]   RSA Factoring Challenge, https://wikimili.com/en/
      RSA_Factoring_Challenge

[2]   Kraft, J. S., & Washington, L. C. (2018). *An introduction to number
      theory with cryptography.* CRC Press, ISBN: 78-1-1380-6347-1.

[3]   Shparlinski, I. (2013). *Finite Fields: Theory and Computation: The Meeting Point of Number Theory, Computer Science, Coding Theory and Cryptography* (Vol. 477). Springer Science & Business Media, ISBN: 978-90-481-5203-2.

[4]   Koblitz, N. (2000). *A survey of number theory and cryptography. In Number Theory* (pp. 217-239). Hindustan Book Agency, Gurgaon.

[5]   Yan, S. Y. (2013). *Computational Number Theory and Modern Cryptography.* John Wiley & Sons, ISBN: 978-1-118-18858-3.

[6]   Atanasiu, A. (2015). *Matematici in criptografie.* US Publishing House, Editor: Universul Stiintific, ISBN: 978-973-1944-48-7.

[7]   Factor Function. Available online: `https://www.mathworks.com/help/matlab/ref/factor.html`

CHAPTER 5

Number Theory

In Chapter 4, we applied number theory to cryptography. Many techniques and tools in cryptography are based on primality, factorization, and radomness, and we have already seen how Euclid's algorithm works. In this chapter, we present in more depth the concepts and ideas behind them, as well as more advanced techniques that deal with characteristics of integer numbers.

This chapter is more technical and contains more mathematics. The definitions and results presented in this chapter are compiled from resources [1]-[5].

Primality and Factorization

We have mentioned the term "prime number" or "prime" a lot in this book. Recall that a prime number is a positive integer that has no divisors except for 1 and the number itself. But how can this be "translated" into a mathematical definition? Mathematically, the definition of a prime number can be one of the following two, discussed next.

Prime Numbers

Let $p \in \mathbb{N}$, $p > 1$. The number p is called prime if:

(a) $(\forall)n \in \mathbb{N}$, $n \mid p \Rightarrow n = 1$ or $n = p$.

(b) $(\forall)a, b \in \mathbb{N}$, $p|ab \Rightarrow p|a$ or $p \mid b$.

These definitions are equivalent. The first definition (a) says that for any positive integer n that divides p, n is 1 or p. In other words, the only divisors of a prime number are 1 and the number itself. The second definition (b) says that a prime number divides a product of two positive integers, and the prime number is one of the two numbers. This is a little more difficult to understand, and it can be seen as related to integer

© Marius Iulian Mihailescu and Stefania Loredana Nita 2021
M. I. Mihailescu and S. L. Nita, *Cryptography and Cryptanalysis in MATLAB*,
https://doi.org/10.1007/978-1-4842-7334-0_5

factorization. The lowest prime number and the only even prime number is $p = 2$. Two integers a, b for which $\gcd(a, b) = 1$ (where gcd is the greatest common divisor) are called *coprime* or *relatively primes*.

A naïve verification for the primality of a positive integer p is to test whether p is divisible by one of the integers $\{2,\ldots,\sqrt{p}\}$. If one number from this set is a divisor of p, then p is not a prime. Listing 5-1 presents this implementation in MATLAB; the result can be seen in Figure 5-1.

Listing 5-1. Checking for Primality

```
1    fprintf('\nTesting the primality of a positive integer...');
2    clear all; close all;
3
4    number = input('\nEnter the number to be tested: ');
5    if number<2
6        disp('The number should be greater than 2. \n');
7        return;
8    end
9
10   if number ~= round(number)
11       disp('The number should be a positive integer. \n');
12       return;
13   end
14
15   if is_prime(number) == 1
16       fprintf('The number %d is prime. \n\n', number);
17   else
18       fprintf('The number %d is not prime. \n\n', number);
19   end
20
21   function check=is_prime(x)
22       check=1;
23       for i = 2:sqrt(x)
24           if mod(x,i) == 0
25               check=0;
26               return;
```

```
27          end
28        end
29    end
```

In the code in Listing 5-1, the user is asked to enter a number (Line 4). The number is verified in certain ways, because it has to meet certain requirements: to be greater than 2 and to be an integer (see Lines 5-13). Checking the primality of a real number, for example, does not make sense. If everything is alright, the is_prime function is called on the number. It is very simple. It just verifies whether the number has divisors in the interval [2, sqrt(*number*)]. If a divisor is found, the for loop is interrupted and we can say for sure that the number is not a prime. Otherwise, if the for loop reaches sqrt(*number*) and no divisor is found, the number is a prime.

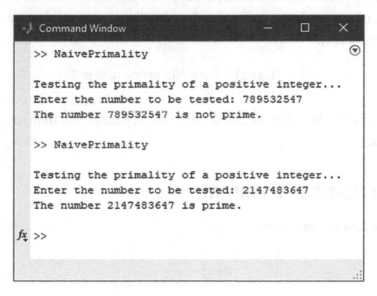

Figure 5-1. *Testing for primality*

Indeed, 789532547 is not prime, because its first divisor (greater than 2) is 17. On the other hand, the primality for the number 2147483647 was proved by Euler in 1772 [9]. This number has the following form:

$$2147483647 = 2^{31} - 1$$

It also is a special number called a *Mersenne prime*. A Mersenne prime has the form $M_n = 2^n - 1$, $n \in \mathbb{N}$, $n > 1$.

There are other, faster techniques for testing the primality, which we will discuss in this chapter. However, there is no known function (and therefore algorithm) that can construct distinct prime numbers.

Regarding prime numbers, there are several conjectures formulated:

- *Goldbach*: Any even number can be written as a sum of two prime numbers.

- *De Polignac:* For any natural number, there exists an infinity number of pairs of prime numbers, such that it is written as the difference between the two primes, i.e., for $(\forall)b \in \mathbb{N}$ there exists an infinity number of pairs (p, q) such that $b = p - q$.

Further, we try to find how dense the set of prime numbers is within the set of natural numbers, or, in other words, the prime number distribution. To do this, we need to define the function $\pi(x)$:

$$\pi : \mathbb{N} \rightarrow \mathbb{N}, \pi(x) = \#\{p \in \mathbb{N} | p \text{ prime and } p \leq x\}$$

In other words, the function counts the number of primes less than or equal to a given number x.

The Prime Number Theorem

The following relationship is true:

$$\pi(x) \sim \frac{x}{\ln(x)}$$

i.e. $$\lim_{x \to \infty} \frac{\pi(x)}{x / \ln(x)} = 1.$$

In other words, the theorem says that $\pi(x)$ is approximated by the number $x/\ln(x)$, where $\ln(x)$ is the natural logarithm, and the approximation becomes more accurate as x increases and approaches ∞. This is also known as the de la Vallee Poussin/Hadamard Theorem (1896), or the conjecture Gauss/Legendre (approx. 1790). Therefore, the prime numbers are distributed asymptotically. This is useful in applications in which we want to know the number of primes lower than a given value.

Next, we discuss congruences and begin by providing the definition of congruency.

Congruency

Let $n, a, b \in \mathbb{Z}$ and $n \geq 2$. We say that a is congruent to b modulo n if $n \mid (a - b)$.

This definition says that a is congruent to b modulo n if the remainders from the Euclidean algorithm (see Chapter 4) for the division between (a and n) and (b and n) are the same. This is denoted with $a \equiv b(mod\ n)$. Sometimes this relationship can be stated as b is a residue of a modulo n. This gives the famous sets denoted with $\mathbb{Z}_n$, which are *congruence classes*. The set $\mathbb{Z}_n$ is defined as $\mathbb{Z}_n = \{0, 1, ..., n - 1\}$. It can be shown that

$$\mathbb{Z}_n = \mathbb{Z} / n\mathbb{Z},$$

where $n\mathbb{Z} = \{..., -1 \cdot n, 0 \cdot n, 1 \cdot n, ...\}$

The tuple $(\mathbb{Z}_n, +, \cdot)$ forms a ring structure, called the ring of integers *modulo n*.

Inverse

In the previous chapter, we computed the modular inverse of a number modulo another number. Here is the formal definition for the inverse of an element *modulo n*:

Let $n \in \mathbb{N}$, $n \geq 2$ and an element $a \in \mathbb{Z}_n$. The inverse of a *modulo n* is the element $b \in \mathbb{Z}_n$ such that $ab \equiv 1(mod\ n)$.

Note that it exists, the inverse is unique, and it is usually denoted with a^{-1}. A very useful relation is given by the following theorem:

Let $n \in \mathbb{Z}$ and $a \in \mathbb{Z}_n$. We say that a is an invertible element in $\mathbb{Z}_n$ iff $\gcd(a, n) = 1$.

Based on this theorem, we computed the modular inverse in the previous chapter.

Chinese Remainder Theorem

Another important theorem that is used often in primitives for cryptography is the Chinese Remainder Theorem, which states the following:

Let $m, n \in \mathbb{N}^*$, $a, b \in \mathbb{Z}$. If m, n are coprime, then $(\exists)x \in \mathbb{Z}$ such that:

$$x \equiv a\,(mod\ m), \quad x \equiv b(mod\ n).$$

Moreover, x is unique when $0 \leq x < mn$.

Primality Tests

We have already seen that in cryptography, prime numbers play a crucial role. Now that we've had a brief introduction to elements of the number theory, we can check whether a number is a prime or a composite. Besides the naïve verification that we implemented previously, there are many more primality tests. If the number is a composite, the next interesting information is its factorization form in prime factors. Primality can be tested using one of the following primality tests:

- Wilson

- Quadratic congruences

- Little Fermat

- Converse Fermat

- Miller-Rabin

- Frobenius

- AKS (Agrawal-Kayal-Saxena)

- Baillie-PSW

- Pollar Rho Test

These tests verify whether the number is a composite rather than verifying its primality 100%. The most commonly used tests are Fermat, Miller-Rabin, and Solovay–Strassen, which we will implement later.

The Wilson Primality Test

This is a very simple test: if p is prime then $(p-1)! \equiv -1 \ (mod \ p)$. The opposite—if $(p-1)! \equiv -1 \ (mod \ p)$ then p is prime—is true for $p \geq 5$. Although it is very simple, it is extremely inefficient, slower even than naïve verification. The implementation in MATLAB is given in Listing 5-2 and the result is shown in Figure 5-2.

Listing 5-2. Implementation of the Wilson Primality Test

```
1    fprintf('\nTesting the primality of a positive integer...');
2    clear all; close all;
3
4    number = input('\nEnter the number to be tested: ');
5    if number<2
6        disp('The number should be greater than 2. \n');
7        return;
8    end
9
10   if number ~= round(number)
11       disp('The number should be a positive integer. \n');
12       return;
13   end
14
15   if is_prime(number) == 1
16       fprintf('The number %d is prime. \n\n', number);
17   else
18       fprintf('The number %d is not prime. \n\n', number);
19   end
20
21   function check=is_prime(x)
22       check=0;
23       fact=factorial(sym((x-1)));
24       if mod(fact+1,x) == 0
25           check=1;
26       end
27   end
```

In the code in Listing 5-2, we made the same verifications for the number that the user introduced. The is_prime function tests whether the number is a prime. This time we initialize the variable check with 0 because we begin with the presumption that the number is not a prime. If the condition is met, check becomes 1 and the number is a prime. Note in this function that we used sym, because the result becomes quite large. For Figure 5-2, we received the answer after about three seconds even though the numbers are really small: 25 and 27. In the naïve verification, we received the answer almost instantaneously and the numbers were a lot larger.

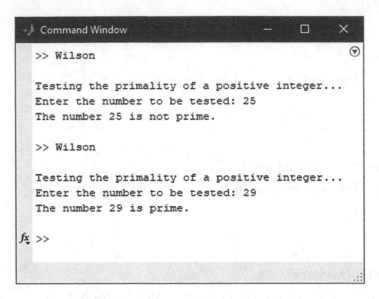

Figure 5-2. *The result of the Wilson primality test*

The Little Fermat Primality Test

This is a probabilistic primality test and it is very simple, having the following description:

1. Choose n, the integer that should be tested.

2. Compute $b = a^{n-1} \, (mod \, n)$, $(\forall) \, a \in \{1, ..., n-1\}$.

3. If $b \neq 1$, then n is not a prime number, which means it is a composite integer.

4. If $b = 1$, $(\forall)b$, then n *may* be a prime number.

Listing 5-3 shows the implementation for Little Fermat; the result is shown in Figure 5-3.

Listing 5-3. Implementation of the Little Fermat Primality Test

```
1   tic;
2   fprintf('\nTesting the primality of a positive integer...');
3   clear all; close all;
4
5   number = input('\nEnter the number to be tested: ');
6   if number<2
7       disp('The number should be greater than 2. \n');
8       return;
9   end
10
11  if number ~= round(number)
12      disp('The number should be a positive integer. \n');
13      return;
14  end
15
16  if is_prime(number) == 1
17      fprintf('The number %d is prime. \n\n', number);
18  else
19      fprintf('The number %d is not prime. \n\n', number);
20  end
21  toc;
22
23  function check=is_prime(x)
24      check=1;
25      for i = 1:(x-1)
26          if mod(power(sym(i),x-1),x)~=1
27              check=0;
28              return;
29          end
30      end
31  end
```

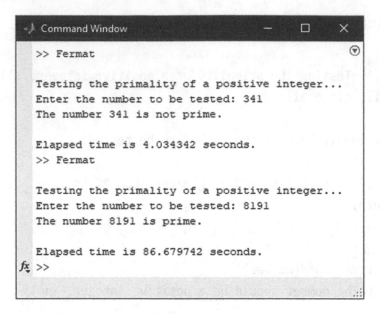

Figure 5-3. *The result of the Little Fermat test*

Verification of primality follows the steps of Little Fermat presented here. We introduced tic at the beginning of the program and toc at the end of the program to measure the time of execution. Note that the time of execution will vary, depending on the machine on which the code runs. The results are indeed correct, because 341 is divisible by 11 and 8191 is the Mersenne number M_{13}.

However, because verifying all numbers between 1 and $n - 1$ is quite expensive, often a number a is chosen for verification, but a should be coprime with n. Here a new term can be introduced, namely *pseudoprime*. The number n is pseudoprime in a base a, where a is coprime with n when $a^{n-1} \pmod{n}$ results in 1 and n is actually not a prime. Little Fermat is typically used when rapid verification of numbers is necessary; for example, it can be used when RSA cryptosystem keys are generated. This approach is given in Listing 5-4.

Listing 5-4. A Variation of the Fermat Primality Test

```
1   tic;
2   fprintf('\nTesting the primality of a positive integer...');
3   clear all; close all;
4
```

```matlab
5    number = input('\nEnter the number to be tested: ');
6    if number<2
7        disp('The number should be greater than 2. \n');
8        return;
9    end
10
11   if number ~= round(number)
12       disp('The number should be a positive integer. \n');
13       return;
14   end
15
16   if is_prime(number) == 1
17       fprintf('The number %d might be prime. \n\n', number);
18   else
19       fprintf('The number %d is not prime. \n\n', number);
20   end
21   toc;
22
23   function check=is_prime(x)
24       check=1;
25       a=generate_coprime(3,x,x);
26       b=mod(power(a,sym(x-1)),x);
27       if b~=1
28           check=0;
29       end
30   end
31
32   function q = generate_coprime(a,b,n)
33       aux=round(a+(b-a)*rand(1,1));
34       while gcd(n,aux)~=1
35           aux=round(a+(b-a)*rand(1,1));
36       end
37       q=aux;
38   end
```

The result of this listing is shown in Figure 5-4. Note the huge difference between the response time. We could even test the number 524287, which is the Mersenne number M_{19}, and the response would be provided in about 17 seconds. The generate_coprime function generates a coprime number with n, in the range $[a, b]$. This range is quite important when we want to avoid false positives, namely to find that n is a prime, when in reality, it is not. This is why we chose the range $[3, n]$ when the coprime was generated (Line 25). An example of false positive is given in [10], where $n = 341$, $a = 2$, and Little Fermat test responds with "is prime" because $2^{340} \equiv 1(mod\ 341)$. However, in fact, 341 is not a prime, because $11 \cdot 31 = 341$.

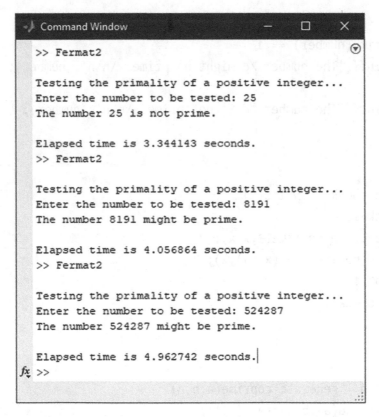

Figure 5-4. *The result of the second approach of the Fermat primality test*

The Miller-Rabin Primality Test

This test is a little more complicated. It has the following description:

1. Choose n, the integer that should be tested.

2. Choose a, such that $a < n$.

3. Write $n - 1$ as $n - 1 = 2^s d$, where d is an odd integer.

4. If the following two conditions are fulfilled, then n is not a prime number:

$$(1) a^d \not\equiv \pm 1 \ (mod \ n)$$

$$(2) a^{2^r d} \not\equiv -1 \ (mod \ n), (\forall) 0 \leq r \leq s - 1$$

In this test, the value a is called a "witness" to the fact of n being composite.

Integer factorization is an important topic in cryptography. It is used to make hardness assumptions about many cryptosystems that are applied to very large numbers, often called "big integers" in programming. MATLAB provides the `factor` function, which breaks a number into its prime factors (see details in Chapter 4).

Algebraic Structures

After that warm up, we can now go further with some information about algebraic structures. We mentioned them when we said that $(\mathbb{Z}_n, +, \cdot)$ is a ring. One of the most commonly used algebraic structures in cryptography is the group. A *group* is a tuple formed from a set G and the operation $\circ$ defined on that set, $(G, \circ)$, with the following rules:

a) $\circ \ : G \times G \to G$

b)   Associativity: $(x \circ y) \circ z = x \circ (y \circ z)$

c)   Neutral element (identity): $(\exists !) e \in G$ *such that* $x \circ e = e \circ x = x$, $(\forall) x \in G$

d)   Inverse: $(\forall) x \in G (\exists !) x^{-1} \in G$ *such that* $x \circ x^{-1} = x^{-1} \circ x = e$

An additional property is

e)   Commutativity: $x \circ y = y \circ x, (\forall) x, y \in G$

47

Note that the element's group identity and the inverse of an element are unique elements. An important point regarding groups is the *order* of the group, which is given by the number of elements of set G, denoted $|G|$ or $\#G$. When $|G| = q$, $q \in \mathbb{N}$, the group has finite order (for example, $(\mathbb{Z}_n, +)$). Otherwise, the group has infinite order (for example, $(\mathbb{Z}, +)$). A group that fulfills condition (d) is called *abelian* or *commutative*. Usually, the operation $\circ$ is the addition or the multiplication; the neutral element is denoted with 0 if the operation is + (addition) and denoted with 1 if the operation is $\cdot$ (multiplication).

Another important property that a group can have is *cyclicity*. A group (G) is cyclic if it is generated by one element, i.e.:

$$G = \left\{ g^n | n \in \mathbb{Z} \right\}$$

However, it is quite difficult for a group to be cyclic, which is why we are very often working with subgroups of a group. A subgroup of a group is defined by the tuple of a subset of G and the same operation defined on G: $(H, +)$, where $H \subseteq G$. An element $g \in G$ can generate a cyclic subgroup of G, as follows:

$$\langle g \rangle \overset{\text{def}}{=} \{ g^n | n \in \mathbb{N} \}$$

The order of an element $g \in G$ is given by the number of elements of the cyclic subgroup that it generates:

$$ord(g) = \langle g \rangle$$

Regarding algebraic structures, there are a lot of results, theorems, and properties that can be applied in cryptography.

In the last decade, many researchers put their efforts into *homomorphic encryption,* a branch of cryptography in which computations can be applied directly over encrypted data. Fully homomorphic encryption is considered the "holy grail of cryptography" [6], because it allows *any* type of computation to be applied an *unlimited* number of times directly over ciphertext and it is considered to be quantum-resistant. Therefore, it is worth mentioning what a homomorphism is.

A *homomorphism* between two groups $(G_1, \star)$, $(G_2, \diamond)$ is a function $\psi : G_1 \to G_2$ with the following property:

$$\psi(x \star y) = \psi(x) \diamond \psi(y), (\forall) x, y \in G_1$$

where $\star$ and $\diamond$ are two binary operations defined over G_1 and G_2, respectively. Note that the function ψ preserves the operation from one group to the other. Usually, these operations are addition and/or multiplication. Examples of cryptosystems that have homomorphic properties are RSA [7] and ElGamal [8] (see details in Chapter 10).

Other important topics regarding homomorphism are the kernel and the image of homomorphism. We will not go into details here, but you can consult the references [1]-[5] for more comprehensive technical information.

Conclusion

In this chapter, you learned that number theory is important in cryptography, because many cryptographic primitives are based on results from it. Prime numbers represent key tools in cryptography and one of the hardness assumptions in cryptography is integer factorization. You learned about some tests that can validate the primality of a given number. In the second part of the chapter, you learned about basic elements of group theory. However, these are just the main mathematical concepts that are used in cryptography. For the comprehensive mathematics behind cryptography, consult the references [1]-[5].

References

[1]   Stinson, D. R., & Paterson, M. (2018). *Cryptography: theory and practice.* CRC press.

[2]   Ferguson, N., & Schneier, B. (2003). *Practical cryptography* (Vol. 141). New York: Wiley.

[3]   Katz, J., & Lindell, Y. (2020). *Introduction to modern cryptography.* CRC press.

[4]   Kraft, J. S., & Washington, L. C. (2018). *An introduction to number theory with cryptography.* Chapman and Hall/CRC.

[5]   Baldoni, M. W., Ciliberto, C., & Cattaneo, G. M. P. (2009). *Elementary number theory, cryptography and codes.* Berlin: Springer.

[6]   Micciancio, D. (2010). *A first glimpse of cryptography's Holy Grail.* Communications of the ACM, 53(3), 96-96.

[7]   Rivest, R. L., Shamir, A., & Adleman, L. (1978). *A method for obtaining digital signatures and public-key cryptosystems.* Communications of the ACM, 21(2), 120-126.

[8]   ElGamal, T. (1985). A *public key cryptosystem and a signature scheme based on discrete logarithms.* IEEE transactions on information theory, 31(4), 469-472.

[9]   Largest known prime number, `https://en.wikipedia.org/wiki/Largest_known_prime_number`

[10] Primality test, `https://en.wikipedia.org/wiki/Primality_test`

CHAPTER 6

Classic Cryptography

This chapter provides an introduction to classic cryptography. It explains the symmetric class of ciphers, whereby the encryption key is the same for both operations—encryption and decryption. Such ciphers are Caesar, Vigenère, Hill, and others. The main goals of this chapter are to give you a clear understanding of the main symmetric cryptographic mechanisms and to provide you with proper implementations in MATALB. These ciphers are not secure and so are not used anymore, but they are good for understanding the main concepts involved in cryptography.

Symmetric Cryptography

Generally speaking, classic cryptography ciphers/algorithms are known as *symmetric* systems. This is because both participants involved in the communication process use the same cryptographic key. Another important aspect, which is vital for the communication (see Figure 6-1), is based on the fact that once you find the encryption key (Enc_k), the decryption key (Dec_k) can be found/computed very quickly by computing the inverse function; see [1] and [2].

Symmetric encryption ciphers can be divided in two main categories: *permutation ciphers* and *substitution ciphers*. A partial list includes the following symmetric algorithms, in ascending order of complexity: the Atbash Cipher, ROT13, the Caesar Cipher, the Affine Cipher, the Polybius Cipher, the Vigenère Cipher, the Hill Cipher, and Playfair. Of course, this list can be improved by adding other classical ciphers and some particular cases of the main ones. A comprehensive list can be seen at [12] and [13]. For more details about symmetric cryptography and algorithms, the following resources should be consulted in parallel: [2], [5], and [6].

51

© Marius Iulian Mihailescu and Stefania Loredana Nita 2021
M. I. Mihailescu and S. L. Nita, *Cryptography and Cryptanalysis in MATLAB*,
https://doi.org/10.1007/978-1-4842-7334-0_6

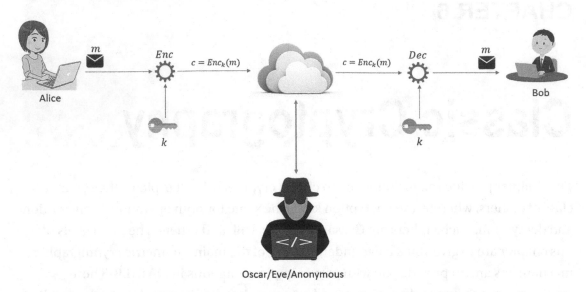

Figure 6-1. *Overview of a practical scenario for symmetric encryption[1]*

Figure 6-1 shows a general scenario that illustrates the communication process in classic cryptography (if it is used in a real communication process). The same key is used by Alice and Bob to encrypt and decrypt the message. If a malicious user gains access to the key, the entire communication process can easily be corrupted.

Classic Ciphers

This section covers the basic implementations in MATLAB of the Caesar, Vigenère, and Hill classic cryptography ciphers.

These implementations are straightforward yet provide the necessary elements for future implementations.

---

[1] Alice, Bob, and Oscar images are downloaded for free from:
```
https://www.kisscc0.com/clipart/computer-icons-user-laptop-personal-computer-
femal-qonpas/
https://publicdomainvectors.org/en/free-clipart/Male-computer-user-vector-
image/70854.html
https://publicdomainvectors.org/en/free-clipart/Spy-behind-computer/68287.html
```

The goal of this section is to provide you with some basic concepts in implementing cryptography algorithms/ciphers, especially using MATLAB. This section can serve as a quick review of the main concepts. As mentioned, these kinds of algorithms/ciphers are not used anymore in real environments, but studying them can help improve your programming skills, in this case, specifically for MATLAB.

The Caesar Cipher

The Caesar Cipher represents one of the simplest and best-known ciphers. It's a substitution cipher, whereby each letter from the plaintext is shifted a certain number of positions (characters) in the alphabet. As an example, if we shift the alphabet two spaces, the letter "A" is replaced with "C," the letter "B" is replaced with "D," and so on. As you will see, the Caesar Cipher is used by other classical ciphers, such as the Vigenère Cipher. The main steps of the Caesar Cipher are included as a step in the Vigenère Cipher. Another cipher that uses the Caesar encryption process is known as ROT13, which uses 13 as the offset.

Example

When we want to send a message from a person to another, the same cryptographic key is used by both partners engaged in this communication process. In the Caesar Cipher, the key is the number of characters used to shift the alphabet.

Example 6-1 represents the encryption and decryption phases involved in the Caesar Cipher. For this, we have chosen a cryptographic key (k) of 3. The text that is encrypted is `welcome to professional cryptography with matlab`.

Example 6-1. Caesar Encryption Procedure

```
plaintext:   welcome to professional cryptography with matlab
ciphertext:  zhofrph wr surihvvlrqdo fubswrjudskb zlwk pdwode
```

As you can see in Example 6-1, the encryption process is very simple, as each plaintext character is shifted in the alphabet by three letters.

The decryption operation is very easy as well, simply using an offset of -3 (see Example 6-2).

Example 6-2. Encryption/Decryption Operations

```
alphabet (plain):    ABCDEFGHIJKLMNOPQRSTUVWXYZ
cipher:              DEFGHIJKLMNOPQRSTUVWXYZABC
```

If a different key is used (except $k = 3$), the decryption will be totally different.

Mathematical Background

The first step translates the characters to numbers (e.g., $a = 0$, $b = 1$, $c = 2$, $d = 3$, $e = 4$, ..., $z = 25$). At this point, we can represent the encryption function for each of the characters from the plaintext as $e(c_i)$, where c_i represents the character we are encrypting. The mathematical function can be represented as follows:

$$e(c_i) = (c_i + k)(mod\ 26)$$

The result of the encryption function is represented by a number that's translated back to a letter. The decryption function is as follows:

$$e(c_i) = (c_i - k)(mod\ 26)$$

Cryptanalysis

It is very easy to crack the Caesar Cipher with the help of automated tools [10]. There are only 25 possible keys representing the alphabet (0-25). Brute-force decryption methods can crack these types of encrypted messages in milliseconds.

A brute-force method determines the fitness value of a chunk of the decrypted text. The process determines if a chunk of encrypted text fits the unencrypted text. It computes the statistics based on the decrypted text and compares those statistics to the ones computed from the standard English text. The fitness function gives us a numeric value, and the higher the value is, the greater probably a particular key is the right one. If you're using this technique, it's best to use quadgram statistics as a fitness measure [9]. The steps are as follows:

- Determine the statistics in the unencrypted text.

- Compute the probability that the ciphertext is the same, using the distribution.

Implementing the Caesar Cipher

Listing 6-1 shows an implementation of the Caesar Cipher. A similar implementation can be found in [7] by Professor Alexander Stanoyevitch. Because the steps of the encryption are quite straightforward and standard, the only different or extra steps that can be added are represented by validating the inputs.

Let's quickly review the implementation of the Caesar Cipher in Listing 6-1. As you can see, the main elements provided by the user are represented by the plaintext that we want to encrypt (the `clear_text` variable in Line 5) and the cryptographic key (the key in Line 8). It is very important to determine the alphabet structure (see Line 2, the `alphabet` variable) before proceeding with the encoding (encryption) phase.

As you can see in Line 10, we are testing if the key is situated between 0 and 26 and in Line 11 there is a modulo computation in Z_{26}.

Line 14 contains a Boolean variable, `breaking_loop`, which is initialized with 0. As the name suggests, the variable is used to exit a loop when criteria is found, after which its value changes to 1 (see Line 20). Another Boolean variable is `iteration_flag`, which is initialized with 1 and declared in Line 16. It's used in a `while` loop (Line 18) to determine if the length of the plaintext entered by the user is less than or equal to 1. Between Lines 23 and 40, the encoding (encryption) process is taking place. As an example, we chose the plaintext `welcometocryptography` and initialized the key with 3. The output is shown in Figure 6-2.

Listing 6-1. Implementation of the Caesar Cipher

```
1    function console_output = caesarcipher()
2
3       alphabet = ['a', 'b', 'c', 'd', 'e', 'f', 'g', 'h', 'i',
4     'j', 'k', 'l', 'm', 'n', 'o','p', 'q', 'r', 's', 't', 'u',
5     'v', 'w', 'x', 'y', 'z'];
6       clear_text = input('Enter a text (plaintext) that you
7     wish to encrypt it (eliminate the spaces): ','s');
8
9       key = input('Enter the key: ');
10
11      if key > 26 || key < 0
12          key = mod(key,26);
13      end
```

```
14
15        breaking_loop = 0;
16        iteration_flag = 1;
17
18      while iteration_flag <= length(clear_text)
19          if ismember(clear_text(iteration_flag),'A':'Z') == 1
20                breaking_loop = 1;
21                console_output = exception_message;
22
23          elseif isletter(clear_text(iteration_flag)) == 1
24                y =
25    strfind(alphabet,clear_text(iteration_flag));
26                z = y+key;
27                  if z > 26
28                      z = z - 26;
29                  end
30                console_output(iteration_flag) = alphabet(z);
31
32          elseif isletter(clear_text(iteration_flag)) == 0
33              if plain(iteration_flag) == ' '
34                  console_output(iteration_flag) =
35      clear_text(iteration_flag);
36              else
37                  breaking_loop = 1;
38                  console_output = exception_message;
39              end
40          end
41
42          iteration_flag = iteration_flag+1;
43          if breaking_loop == 1
44              break
45          end
46      end
47    end
```

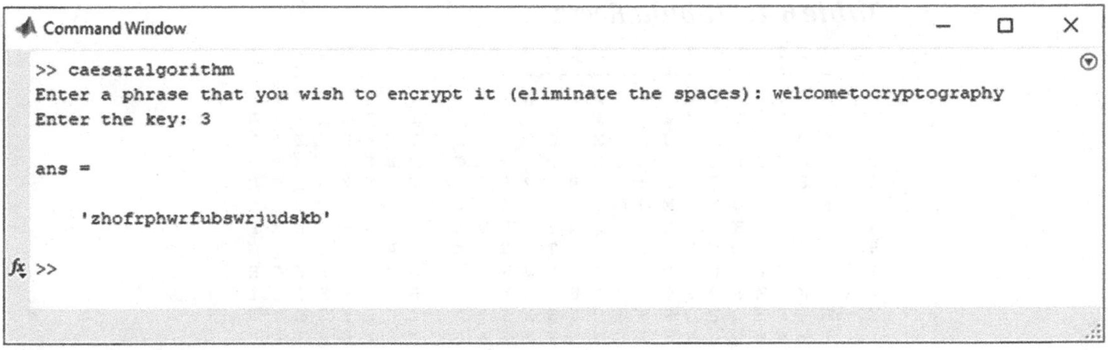

```
Command Window                                                    —    □    ×

>> caesaralgorithm
Enter a phrase that you wish to encrypt it (eliminate the spaces): welcometocryptography
Enter the key: 3

ans =

    'zhofrphwrfubswrjudskb'

fx >>
```

Figure 6-2. *Encryption output of the Caesar Cipher*

The Vigenère Cipher

The Vigenère Cipher is a polyalphabetic substitution cipher. The cipher was considered unbreakable for 300 years, and studies of it are still being published in different journals and conference proceedings.

The first successful attack on the Vigenère Cipher was published in 1863 by Friedrich Kasiski, even though Charles Babbage had designed a successful attack some years before. Another important aspect that is worth mentioning is the fact that Gilbert Vernam worked on the cipher in the early 1900s, proposing and designing what we know now as OTP (One Time Pad). His work had a great impact on current authentication systems.

Example

As an example, we use WELCOME TO THE WORLD OF CRYPTOGRAPHY as the text that we want to encrypt. The cryptographic key is APRESS.

The Vigenère Cipher uses the block in Table 6-1 to encode the plaintext. This table is known as *tabula recta*.

57

Table 6-1. *Tabula Recta*

```
  A B C D E F G H I J K L M N O P Q R S T U V W X Y Z
  ---------------------------------------------------
A A B C D E F G H I J K L M N O P Q R S T U V W X Y Z
B B C D E F G H I J K L M N O P Q R S T U V W X Y Z A
C C D E F G H I J K L M N O P Q R S T U V W X Y Z A B
D D E F G H I J K L M N O P Q R S T U V W X Y Z A B C
E E F G H I J K L M N O P Q R S T U V W X Y Z A B C D
F F G H I J K L M N O P Q R S T U V W X Y Z A B C D E
G G H I J K L M N O P Q R S T U V W X Y Z A B C D E F
H H I J K L M N O P Q R S T U V W X Y Z A B C D E F G
I I J K L M N O P Q R S T U V W X Y Z A B C D E F G H
J J K L M N O P Q R S T U V W X Y Z A B C D E F G H I
K K L M N O P Q R S T U V W X Y Z A B C D E F G H I J
L L M N O P Q R S T U V W X Y Z A B C D E F G H I J K
M M N O P Q R S T U V W X Y Z A B C D E F G H I J K L
N N O P Q R S T U V W X Y Z A B C D E F G H I J K L M
O O P Q R S T U V W X Y Z A B C D E F G H I J K L M N
P P Q R S T U V W X Y Z A B C D E F G H I J K L M N O
Q Q R S T U V W X Y Z A B C D E F G H I J K L M N O P
R R S T U V W X Y Z A B C D E F G H I J K L M N O P Q
S S T U V W X Y Z A B C D E F G H I J K L M N O P Q R
T T U V W X Y Z A B C D E F G H I J K L M N O P Q R S
U U V W X Y Z A B C D E F G H I J K L M N O P Q R S T
V V W X Y Z A B C D E F G H I J K L M N O P Q R S T U
W W X Y Z A B C D E F G H I J K L M N O P Q R S T U V
X X Y Z A B C D E F G H I J K L M N O P Q R S T U V W
Y Y Z A B C D E F G H I J K L M N O P Q R S T U V W X
Z Z A B C D E F G H I J K L M N O P Q R S T U V W X Y
```

The first step is to repeat the keyword above the plaintext (for this demonstration will skip the blank spaces) until it has the same length. It should look like this:

```
Key:        APRESSAPRESSAPRESSAPRESSAPRESSA
Plaintext:  WELCOMETOTHEWORLDOFCRYPTOGRAPHY
```

The procedure to encode the message is based on a simple substitution. It takes each character from the plaintext and locates it on the first column from the table in Figure 6-3, then continues with the first letter from the key and locates it on the first row. Once it identifies the letter from the plaintext on the column and the key on the row, it continues to where they intersect and finds the corresponding letter, as shown in Figure 6-3.

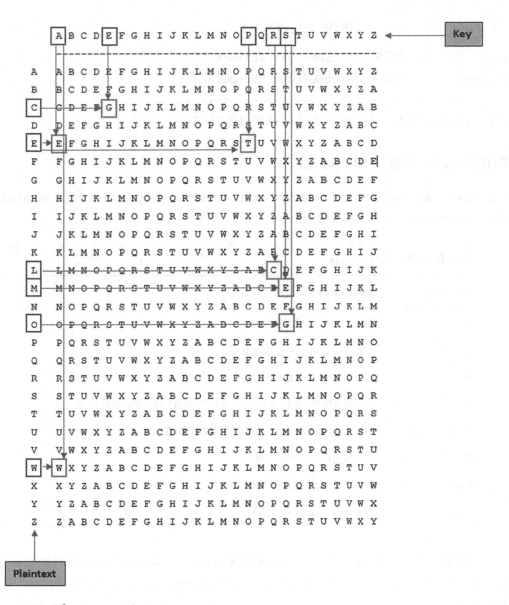

Figure 6-3. *The encryption process*

As an example, we took the first word of the plaintext (WELCOME) and encrypted it using the method described. For the rest of the plaintext, the procedure is the same. The result of the encryption operation is WTCGGEE, as you can see in Figure 6-3.

The encryption of the plaintext is as follows:

```
Key:          APRESSAPRESSAPRESSAPRESSAPRESSA
Plaintext:    WELCOMETOTHEWORLDOFCRYPTOGRAPHY
------------------------------------------------
Encryption:   WTCGGEEIFXZWWDIPVGFRICHLOVIEHZY
```

Mathematical Background

Some important mathematical aspects that are necessary for practical implementations are worth mentioning here; see Table 6-2.

Table 6-2. *Notations*

Notation	Definition
P	The space in the plaintext
C	The space in the ciphertext
K	The space in the keys
$c_1, c_2, \ldots, c_m$	The characters that will be encrypted from the plaintext
$h_1, h_2, \ldots, h_m$	The encrypted values of the characters
k	The cryptographic key
enc_k	The encryption function
dec_k	The decryption function

As a first step, we need to define m as a fixed positive integer. The next step is to define $P = C = K = (Z_{26})^m$. For a specific key, $K = (key_1, key_2, \ldots, key_m)$, let's define the following:

$$enc_K = (c_1, c_2, \ldots, c_m) = (c_1 + key_1, c_2 + key_2, \ldots, c_m + key_m)$$

and

$$dec_K (h_1, h_2, \ldots, h_m) = (h_1 - key_1, h_2 - key_2, \ldots, h_m - key_m)$$

where the entire set of operations is computed in Z_{26}.

Suppose in the following example, $K = (7, 3)$. Let's compute $7^{-1} \bmod 26 = 15$. The encryption function is $enc_k(c) = 7x + 3$, and the decryption function is $dec_k(h) = 15(h - 3) = 15h - 19$.

An important step is to verify if $dec_k(enc_k(c)) = x, \forall c \in Z_{26}$. By performing computations in Z_{26}, we get the following:

$$dec_k\left(enc_k\left(c\right)\right) = dec_k\left(7c + 3\right) = 15\left(7c + 3\right) - 19 = c + 45 - 19 = c$$

Implementing the Vigenère Cipher

Providing an implementation of the Vigenère Cipher is easier than for the Caesar Cipher. Another implementation provided by Professor Alexander Stanoyevitch is shown in [7]. Comparing it with the version provided in Listing 6-2, there are a couple of similarities at first sight. This is due to the main steps of the cipher and the unique way of implementing them, not only in MATLAB but also in other programming languages; see [3], [4], and [6].

The code is self-explanatory. To invoke the encryption function, the user must provide the following call in the Command Prompt (see Figure 6-4):

```
Vigenere_Encryption('welcometocryptography', 'apress')
```

The code from Listing 6-2 has a couple of easy steps; one of the main steps is to convert the encryption key to lowercase letters (see Line 3) and represent them as an array. The next step computes the length of the encryption key (see Line 4). Further, the procedure for encryption is based on computing the modulo operation between the index of each character from the plaintext and the length of the encryption key (see Lines 5 and 6).

Listing 6-2. Implementation of the Vigenère Cipher – Encryption Function

```
1    function output_string =
2    Vigenere_Encryption(plaintext,encryption_key)
3    Array = encryption_key - 'a';
4    keylength = length(encryption_key);
5    for i=1:length(plaintext)
6       ishift = mod(i,keylength);
7       if ishift == 0, ishift = keylength; end
8       output_string(i) =
9    Shift_Encryption(plaintext(i),Array(ishift));
10   end
```

The Shift Encryption function, which is an important function that we kept from [7], is shown in Listing 6-4; its main purpose is to perform the shifting operation, as described in the theoretical background.

Listing 6-3. Shift Encryption Function

```
1    function OutputString =
2    Shift_Encryption(plaintext,moduloInteger)
3    Array = plaintext - 'a';
4    OutputArray = mod( Array + moduloInteger, 26);
5    OutputString = char(OutputArray + 'A');
```

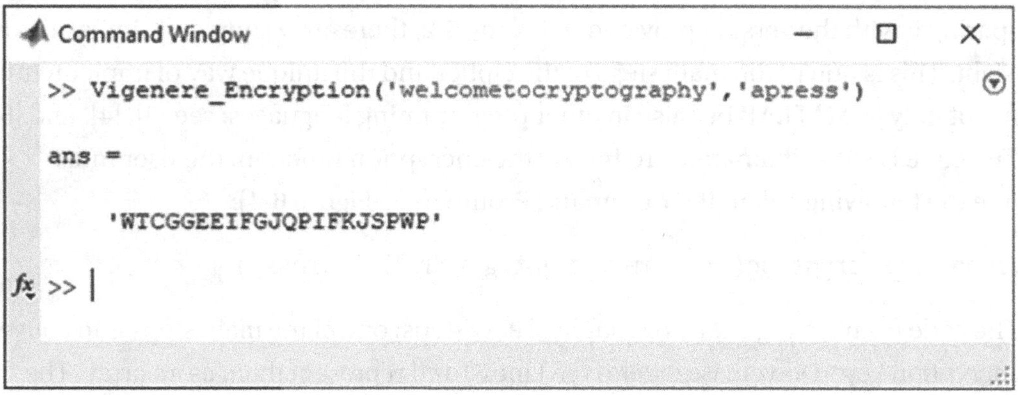

Figure 6-4. *Encryption result of the Vigenère Cipher*

In Listing 6-4, we provide an implementation of the decryption process as being the reverse procedure of encryption. Figure 6-5 shows the output of the decryption function; it is a very good way to check that the encryption function worked as expected.

Listing 6-4. Implementation of the Vigenère Cipher – Decryption Function

```
1    function output_vigenere_decryption =
2    Vigenere_Decryption(plaintext,decryptionKey)
3
4    Array = decryptionKey - 'a';
5    decryption_key = length(decryptionKey);
6    lowercase_string = char((plaintext - 'A') + 'a');
7    for i=1:length(plaintext)
```

```
8      ishift = mod(i,decryption_key);
9      if ishift == 0, ishift = decryption_key; end
10     output_vigenere_decryption(i) =
11           Shift_Encryption(lowercase_string(i),-
12  Array(ishift));
13  end
14  output_vigenere_decryption =
15  char((output_vigenere_decryption - 'A') + 'a');
```

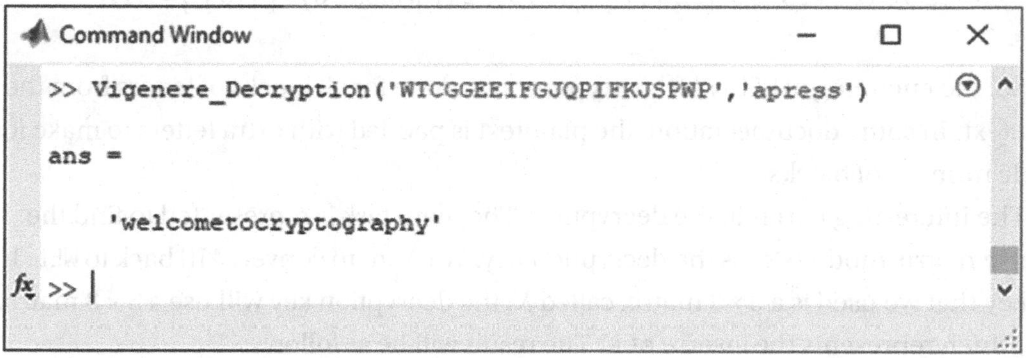

```
Command Window                                    —  □  ×

>> Vigenere_Decryption('WTCGGEEIFGJQPIFKJSPWP','apress')

ans =

    'welcometocryptography'

fx >> |
```

Figure 6-5. *Vigenère Cipher decryption result*

The Hill Cipher

The Hill Cipher was designed in 1929 by Lester S. Hill as a polygraphic substitution cipher based on linear algebra. The main essence of the Hill Cipher is that it uses matrices and matrix multiplication to mix up the plaintext.

The system proposed by Hill was designed to use a series of gear wheels and chains. Unfortunately, the proposed device was never sold.

Example

Most of the Hill Cipher examples use linear algebra and number theory. The key in this encryption process has a matrix structure, as follows:

$$[2\ 6\ 8\ 12\ 14\ 13\ 19\ 9]$$

This example has a size of 3 × 3. It can be any size, as long as the matrix is a square. As an example, let's suppose that you want to encode the message WELCOME TO CRYPTOGRAPHY. To encrypt the message, you need to divide the plaintext into pieces that are three characters/letters long. Let's consider the first three characters/letters from the message (plaintext), WEL, and write them as an array with numeric values that correspond to the letters: $W = 22$, $E = 4$, and $L = 11$.

Once we encode the letters into numbers, we need to do the matrix multiplication as follows:

$$\left[2\,6\,8\,12\,14\,13\,19\,9\,\right]\left[22\,4\,11\,\right]=\left[156\,331\,241\,\right](mod\,26)=\left[0\,19\,7\,\right]=ATH$$

So, the encoding of WEL is ATH. This process is done for all blocks of letters from the plaintext. In some documentation, the plaintext is padded with extra letters to make it a whole number of blocks.

The interesting part is in the decryption. The main task is represented to find the inverse matrix modulo 26 as the decryption key. We want to convert ATH back to WEL. If the key that we used is a 3 × 3 matrix called K, the decryption key will use a 3 × 3 matrix K^{-1}, which represents the inverse of K. The result will be as follows:

$$K^{-1}=\left[0\,19\,7\,\right](mod\,26)=\left[22\,4\,11\,\right]=WEL$$

Cryptanalysis

The Hill Cipher is very vulnerable to a known plaintext attack. Once you know the plaintext and the encrypted version of it, the key can be easily recovered. This is possible because everything is linear.

If you are dealing with a 2 × 2 case of the Hill Cipher, you can launch the attack by computing the frequencies of all the digraphs occurring within the encrypted version of the plaintext. It is very important to understand and to have some familiar knowledge of standard English digraphs, such as "th" and "he". For more information about the cryptanalysis process, resource [8] is recommended, especially for professionals working with old manuscripts, documents, letters, etc.

Implementing the Hill Cipher

Implementing the Hill Cipher in different programming languages (e.g., C#, Java, or C++), as shown in [3] and [4], can be a real adventure due to the multiple steps that need to be achieved. When we are doing the implementation in MATLAB, things are straightforward, as shown in Listing 6-5. A similar version is provided by Professor Alexander Stanoyevitch in [7].

Listing 6-5 shows an example of an encryption function using the Hill Cipher. It is quite similar to [7], because the steps are standard, and the functions can be represented in a unique way. The user invokes the cipher with the following call as input from the Command Prompt:

```
Hill_Encryption('welcome to apress',
                '23 19 12; 0 11 1; 10 18 17')
```

Remember that the matrix given as the second parameter in the call must be inverse modulo Z_{26}.

Let's continue with a quick overview of the source code provided in Listing 6-5. We will start the analysis with Line 2, in which we compute the size of the matrix provided by the user as input (see Figure 6-6). In Line 3, we make sure that all the characters from the plaintext are lowercase letters. Once we have the entire array of characters, in Line 4 we compute the length. In Line 5, we compute a padded value (`append_array_length`) based on the modulo operation between the length of the array (plaintext) and the size of the square matrix (n).

Further, we compute the added length in Line 7 by subtracting the padded value from n. This operation is executed as long as the padded value (`append_array_length`) is greater than 0. In Line 8, we form the new array (plaintext). In Line 11, we compute the number of columns. In Line 12, we compute the reshaped array with the new structure, including the padded value, and in Lines 14 and 15, we output the result of the encryption.

Listing 6-5. The Hill Cipher Encryption Function

```
1    function console_output = Hill_Encryption(plaintext,matrix)
2    [n n] = size(matrix);
3    Array = plaintext - 'a';
4    array_length = length(Array);
```

```
5    append_array_length = mod(array_length,n);
6    if append_array_length > 0
7        add_length = n - append_array_length;
8       Array(array_length + 1: array_length + add_length) = 13;
9    end
10
11   columns_number = length(Array)/n;
12   reshaped_array = reshape(Array, [n columns_number]);
13   ciphertext = mod(matrix*reshaped_array,26);
14   array_output = ciphertext(:)';
15   console_output = char(array_output + 'A');
```

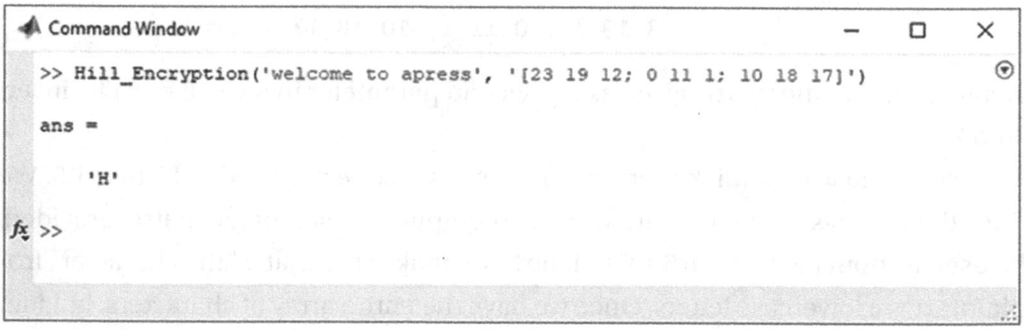

```
▲ Command Window                                              —    □    ×

>> Hill_Encryption('welcome to apress', '[23 19 12; 0 11 1; 10 18 17]')

ans =

    'H'

fx >>
```

Figure 6-6. *Encryption output of the Hill Cipher*

Conclusion

This chapter discussed symmetric cryptography as a main entry point into practical cryptography, providing basic information so you can acquire the basic programming skills you need in MATLAB.

For this purpose, we focused on the Caesar, Vigenère, and Hill Ciphers, as they are well-known ciphers in classic cryptography and are used often during the learning process.

References

[1]   Atanasiu, Adrian. *Securitatea Informației – Volumul 1: Criptografie.* InfoData, 2007. ISBN: 978-973-1803-16-6.

[2]   Menezes, A. J., et al. *Handbook of Applied Cryptography.* CRC Press, 1997.

[3]   Mihailescu, Marius Iulian, and Stefania Loredana Nita. *Pro Cryptography and Cryptanalysis: Creating Advanced Ciphers with C# and .NET.* Apress, 2021. *DOI.org (Crossref)*, doi:10.1007/978-1-4842-6367-9.

[4]   Mihailescu, Marius Iulian, and Stefania Loredana Nita. *Pro Cryptography and Cryptanalysis with C++20: Creating and Programming Advanced Ciphers.* Apress, 2021. DOI.org (Crossref), doi:10.1007/978-1-4842-6586-4.

[5]   Paar, Christof, and Jan Pelzl. *Understanding Cryptography: A Textbook for Students and Practitioners.* Springer Berlin Heidelberg, 2010. *DOI.org (Crossref)*, doi:10.1007/978-3-642-04101-3.

[6]   Schneier, Bruce. *Applied Cryptography: Protocols, Ciphers, and Source Code in C.* 20th anniversary edition, Wiley, 2015.

[7]   Stanoyevitch, Alexander. *Introduction to Cryptography with Mathematical Foundations and Computer Implementations.* CRC Press, 2011. ISBN: 979-8651423514.

[8]   Practical Cryptography (website). Hill Cipher - http://practicalcryptography.com/ciphers/classical-era/hill/.

[9]   Practical Cryptography (website). Quadgram Statistics as a Fitness Measure - http://practicalcryptography.com/cryptanalysis/text-characterisation/quadgrams/.

[10]   Practical Cryptography (website). Cryptanalysis of Caesar Cipher - http://practicalcryptography.com/cryptanalysis/stochastic-searching/cryptanalysis-caesar-cipher/.

[11]   Practical Cryptograhy (website). Caesar Cipher - `http://practicalcryptography.com/ciphers/caesar-cipher/`.

[12]   Practical Cryptography (website). Ciphers - `http://practicalcryptography.com/ciphers/`.

[13]   Cipher Types (website). `https://www.cryptogram.org/resource-area/cipher-types/`.

CHAPTER 7

Pseudo-Random Number Generators

Almost all encryption systems and protocols have a common characteristic: the choice to use arbitrary numbers, apriori unknown and unpredictable. These are called random numbers and they are generated based on statistical context. Random number generators have applications in many domains, such as statistical sampling, computer simulations, or even gambling—any domain in which an unpredictable result is desired.

A series of random numbers can be generated from two main approaches. The first approach measures a physics phenomenon that's expected to be random—these are great sources for natural entropy[1]. The second approach is based on computing algorithms that produce long sequences of numbers that seem to be randomly generated. The second approach results in *pseudo-random* number generators (PRNGs), because the numbers are not truly generated randomly. The algorithms use an initial value called a seed and there is no source of natural entropy, although they may be periodically seeded from natural sources. Another approach in generating pseudo-random numbers is to combine these two main techniques.

Random number generators are useful in developing simulations of the Monte Carlo experiments [1], because the capability of running the same sequence of random numbers based on the same random seed facilitates debugging. This technique can be used in cryptography, as long as the seed remains secret. However, in cryptography, numerical algorithms require a high degree of randomness.

In the context of computing machines, the term *random numbers* refers to a series of bits picked randomly. In statics, there is little information about what random bits could mean. For example, it is known that 0 should be as frequent as 1 is, or 00 should

---

[1] Entropy (information theory), https://en.wikipedia.org/wiki/Entropy_(information_theory)

© Marius Iulian Mihailescu and Stefania Loredana Nita 2021
M. I. Mihailescu and S. L. Nita, *Cryptography and Cryptanalysis in MATLAB*,
https://doi.org/10.1007/978-1-4842-7334-0_7

be chosen half as often as 0 or 1 and just as often as 11, 10, and 01. The randomness "degree" for a series of numbers can be determined using statistical tests. For example, using the Kolmogorov–Smirnov [2] and Diehard [3] tests. In cryptography, it is essential that random numbers be difficult (ideally impossible) to decipher. A perfect random number is the one that an attacker may guess at only by applying brute force. A large part of cryptanalysis is based on exploiting the weaknesses of the functions that generate random numbers.

The most important characteristics of a pseudo-random number generator are the following:

- It should be simple and fast.

- It should output a series of numbers of arbitrary length without repeating numbers. However, a computer can generate numbers smaller than a given value, which means it cannot be designed as a generator with an infinite period. Still, the period should be as high as possible.

- The numbers that it generates should be independent of each other.

- Statistically, numbers should be generated in a uniform distribution.

From the cryptographic point of view, the following two conditions should also be met:

- *Next-bit test* [4]: For any k (representing an arbitrary position in the series of bits generated randomly), if an attacker knows the first k bits in the series (but does not know the seed), the attacker cannot predict the value of the $(k + 1)$th bit in the series by using a polynomial-time algorithm. In [4], it's shown that if a PRNG passes the next-bit test, it also passes in polynomial-time all statistical tests regarding randomness.

- *State compromise extensions*: Even if part of the sequence of pseudo-random numbers is broken or guessed, the whole sequence cannot be deduced/computed.

In cryptography, the "degree" of randomness may vary depending on where the pseudo-random numbers are needed. For example, in some protocols, the generation of a *nonce* should be based on the uniqueness of the nonce, while the generation of a key requires a much higher degree of randomness.

A PRNG can be defined as follows:

(1) Let m, k be two integer numbers, with $m - 1 \geq k > 0$. A (k, m) pseudo-random number generator is a recursive map $f : \mathbb{Z}_2^k \rightarrow \mathbb{Z}_2^m$ that is computed in polynomial time. Usually, m is obtained from k using a polynomial map.

(2) Let S be a sequential circuit with $m = |S|$ states and $F = \{f \mid f : S \rightarrow S\}$ the set of transition functions. A pseudo-random number generator is defined by the relation $x_n = f(x_{n-1})$, where x_0 has some value.

The condition of the security for PRNGs is called the *condition for inseparability*, and it states that for series that are large enough, there is no probabilistic algorithm that can decide whether the series was generated based on the distribution X_n or Y_n. Intuitively, it cannot distinguish between a random distribution and a uniform distribution. There are some standards regarding PRNGS, such as FIPS 186-4 [16], NIST SP 800-90A [17], ANSI X9.17-1985 Appendix C, ANSI X9.31-1998 Appendix A.2.4, ANSI X9.62-1998 Annex A.4, obsoleted by ANSI X9.62-2005, and Annex D (HMAC_DRBG) [18].

Next, we describe the main pseudo-random number generators.

Simple PRNGs

Linear Congruential Generators

An example of congruential PRNG was developed by Lehmer in [5] and is defined by this formula:

$$x_{n+1} = ax_n + b \,(mod\ m),$$

where a, b, m are constant integers, and the seed is an initial value, x_0.

It can be easily observed that a linear congruential PRNG goes into a cycle, whose length is called a *period*, and the maximum period is m. The period m can be achieved by certain values of the pair (a, b). A detailed analysis of this type of generator is found in [6]. The advantage of a linear congruential PRNG is the rapidity of the computations. A general recurrence relationship is:

$$x_{n+k} = \left(a^k x_n + \left(a^k - 1\right)cb^{-1}\right)(mod\ m)$$

which gives a maximum period when:

- $gcd(c, m) = 1$

- $b = a - 1$ is a multiple of p, where p is a prime number that divides by m

- $b \bmod 4 = 0$ if $m \bmod 4 = 0$

The disadvantage of linear congruential PRNGs is that they cannot be used in cryptography. Because we know the first value, it is very easy to compute the rest of the values. The first cryptanalysis for these is presented in [7], where the quadratic and cubic generators were broken, but by now the attack techniques were extended to any linear congruential PRNG.

Ranrot Generators

Initially, the Ranrot class of generator was defined for the Monte Carlo algorithms in [8]. The basis for them is the Fibonacci series, to which is added a shifting operation on bits. There are more types of Ranrot generators [8]:

- Type A: $x_n = ((x_{n-j} + x_{n-k}) \bmod 2^b) \gg r$

- Type B: $x_n = ((x_{n-j} \gg r_1) + (x_{n-k} \gg r_2))(\bmod 2^b)$

- Type B3: $x_n = ((x_{n-i} \gg r_1) + (x_{n-j} \gg r_2) + (x_{n-k} \gg r_3)) \, (\bmod 2^b)$

- Type W: $z_n = \left(\left(y_{n-j} \gg r_3 \right) + \left(y_{n-k} \gg r_1 \right) \right) \left(\bmod \, 2^{\frac{b}{2}} \right)$

$$y_n = \left(\left(z_{n-j} \gg r_4 \right) + \left(z_{n-k} \gg r_2 \right) \right) \left(\bmod \, 2^{\frac{b}{2}} \right)$$

$$x_n = y_n + z_n \cdot 2^{\frac{b}{2}}$$

They have the following conventions:

- All numbers x are binary integers on b bits

- The values i, j, k, n are integer values with $0 < i < j < k \leq n$

- The operation $\alpha \gg s$ is the right-shifting operation with s positions of the α sequence

- For types A, B, and B3, the inequality $0 \leq r_i \leq b - 1$ should be met, while for type W the inequality $0 \leq r_i \leq b/2$ should be met

These values are computed into a buffer vector of k elements called state S_n. The initial state is $S_1 = (x_1, x_2, ..., x_k)$ and passing from one state to the next one is done by a shifting operation to the left of the form $(x_{n-k}, x_{n-k+1}, ..., x_n) \longrightarrow (x_{n-k+1}, ..., x_{n-1}, x_n)$, where x_n is computed based on its type.

Let $p = \gcd(j, k)$. If $p > 1$, then the system can be broken into p subsystems that are independent. Therefore a condition for performance is $\gcd(j, k) = 1$, ensuring in this way the interdependence of all numbers of a state. Similarly, for type W, the number $k - j$ should be a prime. From the method of implementation of the binary addition, it results in a leak of information through the carry bit, beginning from the least significant bits and going to the most significant bits, information that is not carried in the opposite way. To eliminate this issue, several improvements were proposed. For example, add the carry bit to the least significant bit. The best improvement is to shift the bits of the resulting sum. Moreover, to keep the elements from S interdependent, at least one value for r should be non-zero. The maximum length of the period for the Ranrot generator is $(2^k - 1) \cdot 2^{b-1}$. More information about the Ranrot generator can be found in [9].

Blum-Blum-Shub Generator

The simplest and the most efficient PRNG is Blum-Blum-Shub (BBS), also known as the quadratic residual generator [10]. In this PRNG, the Blum integers are used. An integer $n = pq$ is a Blum integer if the prime numbers p and q fulfill the following conditions: $p \equiv 3 \ (mod \ 4)$ and $q \equiv 3(mod \ 4)$. The BBS PRNG has the following steps [10]:

- Let $n = pq$ a Blum, where p and q are prime numbers on $k/2$ bits.

- Let x_0 be a quadratic residual modulo n. The following sequence is defined: $s_{i+1} = s_i^2 \ (mod \ n)$.

- If $z_i = s_i(mod \ 2)$, $1 \leq i \leq m$, then the number generated randomly is $f(x_0) = z_1 z_2 ... z_m$.

As an observation, the bits are not generated recursively, because z_i can be computed directly using the formula $z_i = x_0^{2^i (mod\,(p-1)(q-1))} \bmod 2$ [10]. The hard problem here is the difficulty of factoring n. The value n can be made public, so anyone can generate a sequence of pseudo-random numbers. However, if n cannot be factored, the output cannot be predicted. Moreover, given a part of the sequence, there is no known method of predicting the previous or the next bit. The BBS algorithm is slow, but there are more efficient variations. If n is the length of x_i, then the last $\lfloor \log_2 x_i \rfloor$ bits are kept [11]. At this moment, BBS is considered the most suitable PRNG for protocols of generation and distribution of keys.

Linear Circuit PRNGs

The linear circuits[2] (or *shift registers*) are used in the theory of error detecting and correcting and in some linear encryption systems, such as AES. One of their main advantages is the rapidity of the computations. A linear feedback shift register (LFSR) is a linear circuit formed from a serial register and a feedback function. If the register has n flip-flops of data (DF-F), it will become an n-LFSR. More about shift registers can be found in [12].

One of the more common LFSR PRNGs is the Geffe generator [13], which nonlinearly combines three LFSRs. Cryptographically, this generator does not resist against an attack through correlation. The output of the generator is the same as the output of the second LFSR 75% of the time. Therefore, if the polynomial definitions of the circuits are known, the initial value of the second LFSR and its output sequence can be guessed. Then, the generator counts how many times the output of the second LFSR is the same as the output of the generator. Similarly, the output of the generator is the same as the output of the third generator approximatively 75% of the time [13]. With these two correlations, the sequence can be guessed.

Other LFSR PRNGs are the Stop-and-Go generators:

- *Beth-Piper Generator* [14]: Uses three circuits and controls the clocks of the three circuits. It does not resist an attack through correlation.

- *Gollmann Generator*: [15] Uses a serial cascade of LFSRs, where the clock of the current LFSR is controlled by the clock of the previous LFSR.

---

[2] Circuit, https://en.wikipedia.org/wiki/Circuit_(computer_science)

Other PRNGs

There are many other PRNGs that are based on different mathematical hardness assumptions.

One of them is Blum-Micali PRNG, which is based on the discrete logarithm problem. It uses two prime numbers, p and g, and an initial seed, x_0. The numbers are generated based on the following formula: $x_{i+1} = g^{x_i} \pmod{p}$. The exit from the generator is 1 if $x_i < \dfrac{p-1}{2}$, or 0 otherwise. If p is large enough, the generator is secure.

Another example here is the RSA generator, which is based on the hardness of breaking the RSA encryption system. It uses $n = pq$, where p and q are two large prime integers and e, such that $gcd(e, (p-1)(q-1)) = 1$ and assuming an initial value of $x_0 < n$. The numbers are generated based on the formula $x_{i+1} = x_i^e \pmod{n}$. The exit from the generator is $z_i = x_1 \pmod{2}$. If n is large enough, the generator is secure.

Additional readings about PRNGs are found in [19] and [20].

Practical Implementations

Moving forward with the practical implementations in MATLAB, the pseudo-random numbers are generated using deterministic algorithms [21]. Practically speaking, the numbers are random if they can pass statistical tests with respect to their distribution and correlation [2], [21]. There is a very important separation line between pseudo-random number algorithms and true random numbers; the latter are generated by an algorithm and not by a random method.

The MATLAB random number generators are algorithms used in the process of generating pseudo-random numbers with a specific distribution [21].

As you can observe in [21], the most common methods used in pseudo-random number generation are direct methods, inversion methods, and acceptance-rejection methods.

In the following sections, we provide a couple of standard examples of direct methods (see Listings 7-1 and 7-2 and Figures 7-1 and 7-2) and inversion methods (see Listings 7-3, 7-4, and 7-5 and Figure 7-2), as they are the most common ways to generate pseudo-random numbers.

The direct methods use the distribution [3, 21]. For illustration purposes, we provide a basic, fundamental implementation of a binomial random number generator based on the direct approach (see Listing 7-1). The example in Listing 7-1 is a very basic way to generate random numbers.

Listing 7-1. Binomial Random Number Generator [21]

```
% see [21] for an extended version of this algorithm
function BinomialRandomValue = Listing7_1_DirectMethod_BinomialRandomNumber
Generator(throws,probability,a,b)
% throws - represents the number of throws or tosses
% probability - represents the probability value on a single throw
% a and b - values entered by user, check Listing 7-2 for the example
    BinomialRandomValue = zeros(a,b);
    for k = 1:a*b
        random_value = rand(throws,1);
        BinomialRandomValue(k) = sum(random_value < probability);
    end
end
```

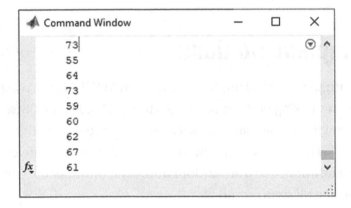

Figure 7-1. *The random values*

To illustrate the example shown in Listing 7-1, we run the script shown in Listing 7-2. It outputs the histogram analysis for the random values. The code is straightforward; it has a default value as the seed for the rng function, based on the values passed as arguments to Listing7_1_DirectMethod_BinomialRandomNumberGenerator. The algorithm in Listing 7-1 computes the binomial random number generator and it will be plotted further with the help of histogram function.

Listing 7-2. Histogram Analysis [21, 15]

```
% see [21] for this sample
rng('default')
binomial_random_value = Listing7_1_DirectMethod_BinomialRandomNumber
Generator(325,0.2,1e7,1);
histogram(binomial_random_value,101)
```

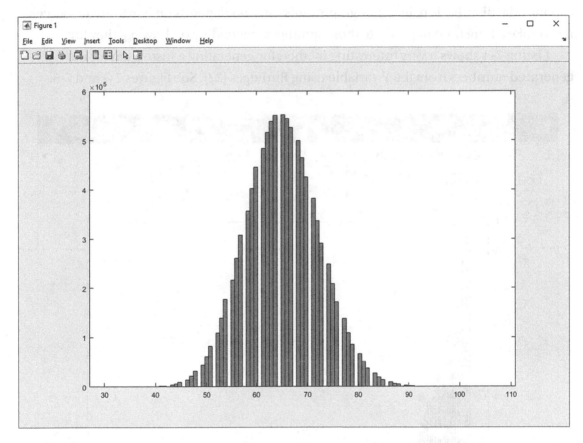

Figure 7-2. *Output of the binomial random number generator [8, 21]*

The next example (see Listing 7-3) demonstrates how to generate random numbers using an exponential distribution [4], [21]. In Listing 7-3, we use the inverse cumulative distribution function [22] and the uniform random number generator, rand [23].

Listing 7-3. Generating Random Numbers Using Exponential Distribution [21]

```
%see [21] for a detailed version
rng('default')
unit = 1;
output = expinv(rand(1e4,1),unit);
```

Listing 7-3 shows the procedure of generating random numbers based on exponential distribution. In cryptography, this method depends on hardware resources. It can take a long time to generate those numbers, depending on how big they are.

Listing 7-4 shows a very interesting method for generating a histogram for the generated numbers from the Y variable using BinEdges [22]. See Figures 7-4 and 7-5.

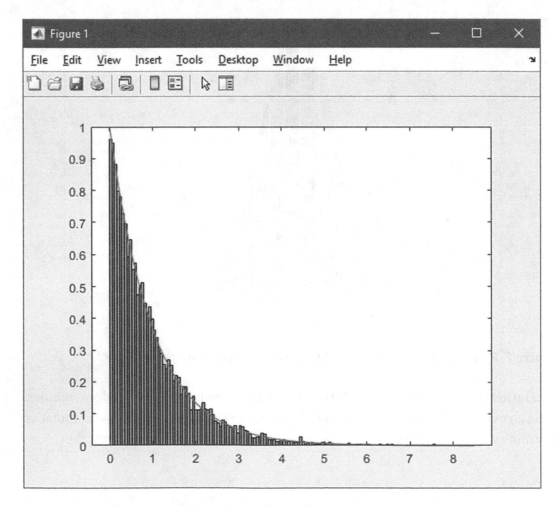

Figure 7-3. *The generated histogram [21, 22]*

Listing 7-4. Generating Histograms of the Generated Numbers of Y Using BinEdges [21, 22]

```
%see [21] for a detailed version

rng('default')
unit = 1;
output = expinv(rand(1e4,1),unit);
Y = output;

numbins = 150;
theHistogram = histogram(Y,numbins,'Normalization','pdf');
hold on
    a = linspace(theHistogram.BinEdges(1),
                theHistogram.BinEdges(end));
    b = exppdf(a,unit);
    plot(a,b,'LineWidth',1)
hold off
```

	Editor - Listing7_4.m				Variables - Y				⊙ ×
Y ×									
⊞ 10000x1 double									
	1	2	3	4	5	6	7	8	9
34	0.0473								
35	0.1022								
36	1.7342								
37	1.1869								
38	0.3814								
39	3.0002								

Figure 7-4. *The Y random values sample*

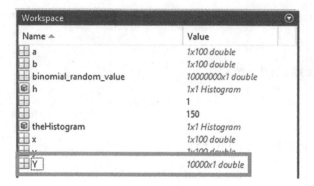

Figure 7-5. *The Y variable initialized in a MATLAB workspace*

Conclusion

In this chapter we have discussed about Psedu-Random Number Generators (PRNGs) and how we can use theoretical concepts and mathematical apparatus in practice. We have covered the most important and simple PRNGs, such as linear congruential generators, ranrot generators, Blum-Blum-Shub generators, linear circuit PRNGs and others.

References

[1]   Kalos, M. H., & Whitlock, P. A. (2009). *Monte Carlo methods.* John Wiley & Sons.

[2]   Massey Jr, F. J. (1951). *The Kolmogorov-Smirnov test for goodness of fit.* Journal of the American Statistical Association, 46(253), 68-78.

[3]   Marsaglia, G. (1996). DIEHARD: a battery of tests of randomness. Available online: `http://stat.fsu.edu/geo`.

[4]   Yao, A. C. (1982, November). *Theory and application of trapdoor functions.* In 23rd Annual Symposium on Foundations of Computer Science (SFCS 1982) (pp. 80-91). IEEE.

[5]   Lehmer, D. H. (1951). *Mathematical methods in large-scale computing units.* Annu. Comput. Lab. Harvard Univ., 26, 141-146.

[6]   Park, S. K., & Miller, K. W. (1988). *Random number generators: good ones are hard to find.* Communications of the ACM, 31(10), 1192-1201.

[7]   Plumstead, J. B. (1982, November). *Inferring a sequence generated by a linear congruence.* In 23rd Annual Symposium on Foundations of Computer Science (sfcs 1982) (pp. 153-159). IEEE.

[8]   Fog, A. (2001). Chaotic random number generators with random cycle lengths. Available online: `http://www.agner.org/random/theory/chaosran.pdf`.

[9]   Fog, A. Theory articles. Available online: `https://www.agner.org/random/theory/`

[10]   Blum, L., Blum, M., & Shub, M. (1986). *A simple unpredictable pseudo-random number generator.* SIAM Journal on computing, 15(2), 364-383.

[11]   Sidorenko, A., & Schoenmakers, B. (2005, December). *Concrete security of the Blum-Blum-Shub pseudorandom generator.* In IMA International Conference on Cryptography and Coding (pp. 355-375). Springer, Berlin, Heidelberg.

[12]   Goresky, M., & Klapper, A. (2012). *Algebraic shift register sequences.* Cambridge University Press.

[13]   Wei, S. (2006). *On generalization of Geffe's generator.* IJCSNS International Journal of Computer Science and Network Security, 6(8A), 161-165.

[14]   Beth, T., & Piper, F. (1984, April). *The Stop-and-Go Generator.* In Eurocrypt (Vol. 84, pp. 88-92).

[15]   Park, S. J., Lee, S. J., & Goh, S. C. (1995, August). *On the security of the Gollmann cascades.* In Annual International Cryptology Conference (pp. 148-156). Springer, Berlin, Heidelberg.

[16]   FIPS PUB 186-4, Available online: `https://nvlpubs.nist.gov/nistpubs/FIPS/NIST.FIPS.186-4.pdf`

[17]   NIST 800-90A Rev. 1, Available online: https://csrc.nist.gov/
publications/detail/sp/800-90a/rev-1/final

[18]   Random Bit Generation, Available online: https://csrc.nist.
gov/projects/random-bit-generation

[19]   Everest, G., Van Der Poorten, A. J., Shparlinski, I., & Ward, T. (2003).
Recurrence sequences (Vol. 104). Providence, RI: American
Mathematical Society.

[20]   Bassham III, L. E., Rukhin, A. L., Soto, J., Nechvatal, J. R., Smid,
M. E., Barker, E. B., ... & Vo, S. (2010). Sp 800-22 rev. 1a. *A statistical
test suite for random and pseudorandom number generators for
cryptographic applications*. National Institute of Standards &
Technology.

[21]   Generating Pseudo-Random Numbers. Available online: https://
www.mathworks.com/help/stats/generating-random-data.
html.

[22]   Cummulative Distribution Function. Available online: https://
www.mathworks.com/help/stats/prob.normaldistribution.
cdf.html.

[23]   Uniformly Distributed Random Numbers. Available online:
https://www.mathworks.com/help/matlab/ref/rand.html.

[24]   BinEdges. Available online: https://www.mathworks.com/help/
matlab/ref/matlab.graphics.chart.primitive.histogram.
html.

CHAPTER 8

Hash Functions

A hash function is a function that has the potential to map data of an arbitrary size to values that have a fixed size. The output of a hash function is known as a *hash value, hash code, digest, or hash.*

The values obtained as output are used to index a fixed-size table, known as *hash table.* The process of using a hash function to index a hash table is known as *hashing* or *scatter storage addressing.*

The goal of a hash function is essentially to guarantee the integrity of a message. With its help, developers can build a "digital mark" of the message, which, by period checking, they can certify if it is modified.

Hash function class. A hash class is represented as a quadruple (M, D, K, H), where:

- M represents the set of possible messages (encrypted or not)

- D represents a finite set of digital marks (or digested)

- K represents a finite set of keys

- For each of $k \in K$, there is a hash function, $h_k \in H$, $h_k : M \to Y$

The idea of a hash comes from the fact that, although M can be a very large , Y is a finite set. We always have $card(M) \geq card(D)$. Almost all the applications will request a strong condition: $card(M) \geq 2 \cdot card(D)$.

A pair of $(m, d) \in M \times D$ is valid for K if $h_k(m) = y$.

M. I. Mihailescu and S. L. Nita, *Cryptography and Cryptanalysis in MATLAB,*
https://doi.org/10.1007/978-1-4842-7334-0_8

Security of Hash Functions

This section discusses the general ideas of hash functions, such as the security of hash functions, birthday attack/paradox, and the applications of hash functions.

Before proceeding with the implementation of the hash functions, we need to cover a few theoretical points. As mentioned in other works, such as [2] and [3], cryptography is almost impossible without the basic theoretical ideas. It is very important to know what you are doing when you provide an implementation, especially if the implementation is from scratch and you are not using third-party libraries, SDKs, or scripts from the Internet without properly verifying the source code.

Cryptographic Hash Functions

Here we have a single hash function $h : M \to D$. From a security point of view (cryptographic), the only way to obtain a valid pair $(m, d) \in M \times D$ is to choose m and to compute $d = h(m)$. To achieve this, the computation will face the following three difficult problems:

- *Non-reversible*: When $d \in D$, it is difficult to find $m \in M$ in such a way that $d = h(m)$.

- *Weak collisions*: If we have a valid pair (m, d), it is difficult to find $m_1 \neq m$ with $h(m_1) = h(m)$.

- *Collisions*: It is difficult to find two distinct values $m, m_1 \in M$ in such a way that $h(m) = h(m_1)$.

Note that the collisions problem will not lead directly to a valid pair. Also, if (m, d) is a valid pair and (m, m_1) is a collision, then (m_1, d) is a valid pair as well.

A *hash function* $h : M \to D$ for which the collisions problem is difficult is called collision resistant.

Because $card(M) > card(D)$, any hash function admits collisions. If a hash function is resistant to collisions, the function will resist weak collisions. In this case, *collisions* involve *weak collisions*.

Suppose that we have a hash function defined as $h : M \to D$, where M, D are finite sets, $card(M) \geq 2 \cdot card(D)$. Suppose that we have an algorithm Q that represents the inverse of h. There will then be a probabilistic algorithm that will find a collision for h with the probability of $\frac{1}{2}$.

Suppose that we have the inversion algorithm Q for the inversion of h, which is represented as an oracle A, which admits as input a mark $m \in M$. It will return an element $Q(d) \in M$, in such a way that $h(Q(d)) = d$. Next, we consider the following algorithm, which is noted with W:

1. $m \in M$ is randomly choosen

2. $d \leftarrow h(m)$

3. $m_1 \leftarrow Q(d)$

4. *if* $m_1 \neq x$ then m_1 and m represents a collision for h with success

5. else end

Algorithm W is a probabilistic algorithm that will return a collision or no answer. So, in this case, it's quite sufficient to compute the success probability.

Birthday Attack

A *birthday attack* is a simple method for obtaining collisions. The name comes from the birthday paradox. In a simplified version, it can be stated as follows: *the probability of having two people with the same birthday from a randomly set of 23 people is at least* $\frac{1}{2}$.

Consider two finite sets, M and D, with $card(M) \geq 2 \cdot card(D)$ and a hash function defined as $h : M \rightarrow D$. It is easy to show that we have $card(M)$ collisions. The main problem is to highlight those collisions.

A simple method is based on randomly extracting f distinct messages $f_1, ..., f_k \in M$. Next, compute $d_i = h(m_i)$, $1 \leq i \leq k$ and see if there is a collision between them. This is achieved by sorting the d_i values.

As m_i are randomly extracted, d_i can be considered random elements, not necessarily distinct from D. The probability from p extractions that all the elements d_i are distinct is determined as follows: A sort of the numbers d_i is done in $d_1, ..., d_p$ order. The first extraction d_1 is random; the probability of $d_2 \neq d_1$ is $1 - \frac{1}{card(M)}$, and the probability of d_3 to be distinct from d_1 and d_2 is $1 - \frac{2}{card(M)}$.

The probability to show that we don't have any collisions, is as follows:

$$\left(1 - \frac{1}{card(M)}\right)\left(1 - \frac{2}{card(M)}\right) \cdots \left(1 - \frac{p-1}{card(M)}\right) = \prod_{i=1}^{p-1}\left(1 - \frac{i}{card(M)}\right)$$

If m is a real number, we can use the approximation. The current approximation is obtained from the Maclaurin Series [1] (Listing 8-1 shows a MATLAB implementation).

Listing 8-1. Implementation of the Maclaurin Series

```
1    function Listing81
2    n=5;
3    x=input ('Give a value X = ')
4    e_s=(0.3*13^(4-n))
5    e=100
6    ml(1)=1
7    it=1
8    while e>e_s
9    it=it+1
10   ml(it)=ml(it-1)+(x)^(it-1)+x^(2+(it-1))/factorial(2+(it-1))
11   e=abs((ml(it)-ml(it-1))/ml(it))
12   end
13
14   disp(['number of iterations= ',num2str(it)])
15   disp(['epsilon= ',num2str(e)])
```

In Line 3, we define a variable x that will store the numeric value given by the user, and that represent the seed value for which we will compute the e_s, epsilon series. In Line 5, the e variable (the epsilon maximum value) is initialized with 100.

In Lines 6 and 7, we can see that the first element of the Maclaurin Series, ml, is initialized with 1. Next, the iteration it is initialized with 1. Lines 9 - 11 are executed as long as the while instruction in Line 8 is true. In Line 10, we execute the Maclaurin Series for the current iteration value. The final value of the iterations is shown in Line 14. In Line 11, we compute the absolute value for the epsilon variable, which is displayed in Line 14. For more details, see Figure 8-1.

```
Command Window                                                              —  □  ×
    0.0000    0.0000    0.0000    0.0000    0.0000    0.0000    0.0000    0.0000    0.0000    0.0000    0.0000    0.0000

Columns 301 through 312

    0.0000    0.0000    0.0000    0.0000    0.0000    0.0000    0.0000    0.0000    0.0000    0.0000    0.0000    0.0000

Columns 313 through 324

    0.0000    0.0000    0.0000    0.0000    0.0000    0.0000    0.0000    0.0000    0.0000    0.0000    0.0000    0.0000

Columns 325 through 336

    0.0000    0.0000    0.0000    0.0000    0.0000    0.0000    0.0000    0.0000    0.0000    0.0000    0.0000    0.0000

Columns 337 through 348

    0.0000    0.0000    0.0000    0.0000    0.0000    0.0000    0.0000    0.0000    0.0000    0.0000    0.0000    0.0000

fx  Columns 349 through 360
```

Figure 8-1. *Maclaurin Series output*

The birthday attack is a brute-force attack that tries to find collisions. Generally speaking, *Oscar/Eve* will randomly generate some messages m_1, m_2, ...$m_n \in M$. For each of the messages m_i it will compute and store the mark $d_i = h(m_i)$, comparing the mark with the previous stored value. If $h(m_i)$ is the same as another value $h(m_j)$ that is stored, it means that *Oscar/Eve* have found a collision (m_i, m_j). According to the paradox, this can happen after $2 \frac{card(M)}{2}$ messages.

For an implementation of the birthday attack, see Listing 8-2 and Figure 8-2.

Listing 8-2. Implementation of the Birthday Attack

```
1    clear; clc;
2    random_group_people = 100;
3    A = ones(100, random_group_people);
4    probability = 1;
5       for i = 1 : 100
6           A(i) = 1 - probability;
7           probability = probability * (365 -i)/365;
8       end
9
10   plot(A, 'green')
11   title('The probability that two people to have the same
12   birthday from a group of 100 people');
13   xlabel('The size of the group of people');
14   ylabel('Probability for the same birthday');
```

Let's quickly examine the algorithm in Listing 8-2 and see how such an algorithm would work in a real-life scenario.

In Line 2, we randomly choose a group of 100 people. In Line 3, we declare a matrix of 100 × 100, which will be initialized with 1. In Line 4, we set the probability to 1 and in Lines 6 and 7 we initialize each element of the matrix A with 1-probability. In Line 7 we reinitialize the probability with minus a unit (person). We can see that in Line 5, the `for` goes from 1 to 100 for each person.

In Line 10, we plot the curve and show the probability as a graphic (see Figure 8-2). Lines 11, 12, 13, and 14 show the configuration of the diagram, including the labels for the *x* and *y* axes and the title.

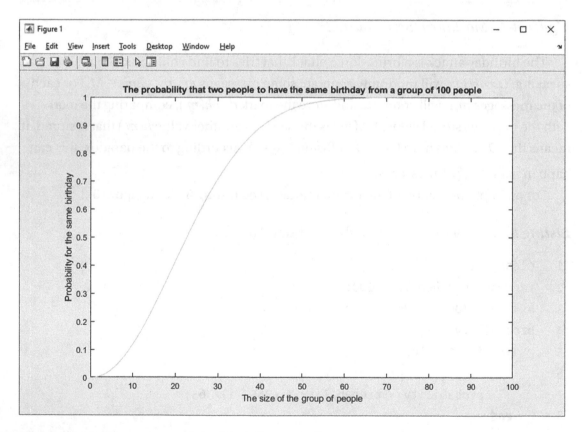

Figure 8-2. *The output of the birthday paradox*

MD4 Function

MD (Message Digest) functions were built and designed by Ron Rivest. MD4 was introduced in 1990 [4] and was used on 32-bit processors. Although the function was not secure enough, the basic principles were used later in a large class of hash functions, including MD5, SHA, SHA1, and RIPEMD160. Their security was not proved, and the attacks that took place pointed out different weaknesses in their construction. However, the MD functions have the advantage of being very fast and practical for signing long messages.

MD4 Function Description

Let's consider a string $y \in Z_2^*$. We will define the following table $T = T_0 T_1 ... T_{n-1}$ with each T_i (called and known as the word) of length 32 and $g \equiv 0 \ (mod \ 16)$. T is built using Algorithm 8-1.

Algorithm 8-1. Building the T Table

1. $d \leftarrow (447 - |y|)(mod \ 512)$

2. $f \leftarrow binary \ representation \ of \ |y| \ (mod \ 2^{64}), where \ |s| = 64$

3. $T = y \ \| \ 1 \ \| \ 0e \ \| \ s$

MD4 will build a mark of y of 128 bits. Algorithm 8-2 generates the mark. Algorithm 8-2 is the main essence of MD4 implemented in MATLAB or any other programming language.

Algorithm 8-2. MD4 Building the Mark of y

1. $W_1 \leftarrow (67452301)_{16}$,

$$W_2 \leftarrow (efcdab89)_{16}, \ W_3 \leftarrow (98badcfe)_{16}, \ W_4 \leftarrow (10325476)_{16}$$

2. $for \ i = 0 \ to \dfrac{n}{16} - 1 \ do$

    a. $for \ j = 0 \ to \ 15 \ do \ Y_i \leftarrow T_{16i} + j$

        i. $W_1 W_1 \leftarrow W_1 \quad W_2 W_2 \leftarrow W_2 \quad W_3 W_3 \leftarrow W_3 \quad W_4 W_4 \leftarrow W_4$

        ii. Phase 1

        iii. Phase 2

    iv. Phase 3

    v. $W_1 \leftarrow W_1 + W_1W_1, \quad W_2 \leftarrow W_2 + W_2W_2, \quad W_3 \leftarrow W_3 + W_3W_3,$
        $W_4 \leftarrow W_4 + W_4W_4$

The mark $h(y)$ represents the concatenation of the words W_1, W_2, W_3, and W_4, which are known as *registers* as well. The algorithm will split the table M into strings of 16 consecutive words, for which three phases are applied. The adding operation in step v are done in modulo 2^{32}.

Consider $\theta, \phi \in Z_2^*$, $|\theta| = |\phi|$. The three phases are based on the following operations:

- $\theta \wedge \phi$ and logic bit by bit (AND)

- $\theta \vee \phi$ or logic bit by bit (OR)

- $\theta \bigoplus \phi$ or exclusive bit by bit (XOR)

- $\theta + \phi$ modulo addition 2^{32}

- $\theta \ll s$ cyclic shifting with s bits to the left $(1 \leq s \leq 31)$

- $\neg\theta$ cyclic shifting with s bits to the left $(1 \leq s \leq 31)$

The default construction of MD4 is based on the little-endian architecture. Because the mark resulted by the process of hashing has to be independent from the computer's architecture, for an implementation of MD4 on a big-endian computer, the additions will be defined as follows:

- Perform interchange for $y_1 \leftrightarrow y_4$, $y_2 \leftrightarrow y_3$, $z_1 \leftrightarrow z_4$, $z_2 \leftrightarrow z_3$

- Compute $L = G + V \ (mod \ 2^{32})$

- Perform interchange $r_1 \leftrightarrow r_4$, $r_2 \leftrightarrow r_3$

The three phases for construction of MD4 hash function are $\delta, \vartheta, \xi : Z_2^{32} \times Z_2^{32} \times Z_2^{32} \to Z_2^{32}$ defined as:

- $\delta(G, V, L) = (G \wedge V) \vee ((\neg X) \wedge Z)$

- $\vartheta(G, V, L) = (G \wedge V) \vee (G \wedge L) \vee (V \wedge L)$

- $\xi(G, V, L) = G \oplus V \oplus L$

The description of the three phases is as follows. The following phases are found in the implementation. Practically speaking, the following phases are found in the core of the MD4 hash function.

Phase 1

1. $W_1 \leftarrow (W_1 + \delta(W_2, W_3, W_4) + X_0 \lll 3$
2. $W_4 \leftarrow (W_4 + \delta(W_1, W_2, W_3) + X_1 \lll 7$
3. $W_3 \leftarrow (W_3 + \delta(W_4, W_1, W_2) + X_2 \lll 11$
4. $W_2 \leftarrow (W_2 + \delta(W_3, W_4, W_1) + X_3 \lll 19$
5. $W_1 \leftarrow (W_1 + \delta(W_2, W_3, W_4) + X_4 \lll 3$
6. $W_4 \leftarrow (W_4 + \delta(W_1, W_2, W_3) + X_5 \lll 7$
7. $W_3 \leftarrow (W_3 + \delta(W_4, W_1, W_2) + X_6 \lll 11$
8. $W_2 \leftarrow (W_2 + \delta(W_3, W_4, W_1) + X_7 \lll 19$
9. $W_1 \leftarrow (W_1 + \delta(W_2, W_3, W_4) + X_8 \lll 3$
10. $W_4 \leftarrow (W_4 + \delta(W_1, W_2, W_3) + X_9 \lll 7$
11. $W_3 \leftarrow (W_3 + \delta(W_4, W_1, W_2) + X_{10} \lll 11$
12. $W_2 \leftarrow (W_2 + \delta(W_3, W_4, W_1) + X_{11} \lll 19$
13. $W_1 \leftarrow (W_1 + \delta(W_2, W_3, W_4) + 12 \lll 3$
14. $W_4 \leftarrow (W_4 + \delta(W_1, W_2, W_3) + X_{13} \lll 7$
15. $W_3 \leftarrow (W_3 + \delta(W_4, W_1, W_2) + X_{14} \lll 11$
16. $W_2 \leftarrow (W_2 + \delta(W_3, W_4, W_1) + X_{15} \lll 19$

Phase 2

1. $W_1 \leftarrow (W_1 + \vartheta(W_2, W_3, W_4) + X_0 + P \lll 3$
2. $W_4 \leftarrow (W_4 + \vartheta(W_1, W_2, W_3) + X_4 + P \lll 5$
3. $W_3 \leftarrow (W_3 + \vartheta(W_4, W_1, W_2) + X_8 + P \lll 9$
4. $W_2 \leftarrow (W_2 + \vartheta(W_3, W_4, W_1) + X_{12} + P \lll 13$
5. $W_1 \leftarrow (W_1 + \vartheta(W_2, W_3, W_4) + X_1 + P \lll 3$
6. $W_4 \leftarrow (W_4 + \vartheta(W_1, W_2, W_3) + X_5 + P \lll 5$
7. $W_3 \leftarrow (W_3 + \vartheta(W_4, W_1, W_2) + X_9 + P \lll 9$
8. $W_2 \leftarrow (W_2 + \vartheta(W_3, W_4, W_1) + X_{13} + P \lll 13$

9. $W_1 \leftarrow (W_1 + \vartheta(W_2, W_3, W_4) + X_2 + P \lll 3$

10. $W_4 \leftarrow (W_4 + \vartheta(W_1, W_2, W_3) + X_6 + P \lll 5$

11. $W_3 \leftarrow (W_3 + \vartheta(W_4, W_1, W_2) + X_{10} + P \lll 9$

12. $W_2 \leftarrow (W_2 + \vartheta(W_3, W_4, W_1) + X_{14} + P \lll 13$

13. $W_1 \leftarrow (W_1 + \vartheta(W_2, W_3, W_4) + X_3 + P \lll 3$

14. $W_4 \leftarrow (W_4 + \vartheta(W_1, W_2, W_3) + X_7 + P \lll 5$

15. $W_3 \leftarrow (W_3 + \vartheta(W_4, W_1, W_2) + X_{11} + P \lll 9$

16. $W_2 \leftarrow (W_2 + \vartheta(W_3, W_4, W_1) + X_{15} + P \lll 13$

where $P = 5a827999$

Phase 3

1. $W_1 \leftarrow (W_1 + \xi(W_2, W_3, W_4) + X_0 + P \lll 3$

2. $W_4 \leftarrow (W_4 + \xi(W_1, W_2, W_3) + X_8 + P \lll 9$

3. $W_3 \leftarrow (W_3 + \xi(W_4, W_1, W_2) + X_4 + P \lll 11$

4. $W_2 \leftarrow (W_2 + \xi(W_3, W_4, W_1) + X_{12} + P \lll 15$

5. $W_1 \leftarrow (W_1 + \xi(W_2, W_3, W_4) + X_2 + P \lll 3$

6. $W_4 \leftarrow (W_4 + \xi(W_1, W_2, W_3) + X_{10} + P \lll 9$

7. $W_3 \leftarrow (W_3 + \xi(W_4, W_1, W_2) + X_6 + P \lll 11$

8. $W_2 \leftarrow (W_2 + \xi(W_3, W_4, W_1) + X_{14} + P \lll 15$

9. $W_1 \leftarrow (W_1 + \xi(W_2, W_3, W_4) + X_1 + P \lll 3$

10. $W_4 \leftarrow (W_4 + \xi(W_1, W_2, W_3) + X_9 + P \lll 9$

11. $W_3 \leftarrow (W_3 + \xi(W_4, W_1, W_2) + X_5 + P \lll 11$

12. $W_2 \leftarrow (W_2 + \xi(W_3, W_4, W_1) + X_{13} + P \lll 15$

13. $W_1 \leftarrow (W_1 + \xi(W_2, W_3, W_4) + X_3 + P \lll 3$

14. $W_4 \leftarrow (W_4 + \xi(W_1, W_2, W_3) + X_{11} + P \lll 9$

15. $W_3 \leftarrow (W_3 + \xi(W_4, W_1, W_2) + X_7 + P \lll 11$

16. $W_2 \leftarrow (W_2 + \xi(W_3, W_4, W_1) + X_{15} + P \lll 15$

where $P = 6ed9eba1$

Cryptanalysis of MD4

The phases of MD4 function are characterized by permutations λ_i of the block $G = (G_0, ..., G_{15})$ and cyclic shifting to the left $\theta_{i,j}$, $i = 1, 2, 3, ..., 16$ and $j = 1, 2, 3, ..., 16$.

The three permutations applied to all three phases are as follows:

$$\lambda_1 = (0\,1\,2\,3\,4\,5\,6\,7\,8\,9\,10\,11\,12\,13\,14\,15\,0\,1\,2\,3\,4\,5\,6\,7\,8\,9\,10\,11\,12\,13\,14\,15\,)$$

$$\lambda_2 = (0\,1\,2\,3\,4\,5\,6\,7\,8\,9\,10\,11\,12\,13\,14\,15\,0\,4\,8\,12\,1\,5\,9\,13\,2\,6\,10\,14\,3\,7\,11\,15\,)$$

$$\lambda_3 = (0\,1\,2\,3\,4\,5\,6\,7\,8\,9\,10\,11\,12\,13\,14\,15\,0\,8\,4\,12\,2\,10\,6\,14\,1\,9\,5\,13\,3\,11\,7\,15\,)$$

Formally, an attack on an MD4 hash function for the first two phases is as follows:

1. *Input*: W_1, W_2, W_3, W_4

2. *for* $i = 0,1,2,4,5,6,8,9,10,12,13$ *do* $G_{\sigma_2^{-1}(i)} \leftarrow -P$

3. *for* $i = 12$ *to* 14 *do*

4. $G_i \leftarrow -(W_1 + \delta(W_2, W_3, W_4))$

5. $(W_1, W_4, W_3, W_2) \leftarrow (W_4, W_3, W_2, 0)$

6. $W_2 \leftarrow W_1$

7. *if* $u(G_{15}) = u(G'_{15})$ *then*

8. $G'_i = G_i \quad (0 \leq i \leq 14)$

9.   *Output*(G, G');   *Exit*

10.

11. Function $u(G_{15})$

12. $W_1 \leftarrow 0, C \leftarrow 0, D \leftarrow 0$;

13. $W_2 \leftarrow ((W_{20} + G_{15} + P) \lll \theta_{1,15})$;

14. *for* $i = 0$ *to* 15 *do*

15. $(W_1, W_4, W_3, W_2) \leftarrow (W_4, W_3, W_2, (W_1 + \vartheta(W_2, W_3, W_4) + G_{\sigma_2(i)} + P) \lll \theta_{2,i}$

16. *Return* (W_2)

MD5 Function

In 1992, Rivest proposed a better version of MD4, called MD5. It was published under RFC 1321 Internet Standard [5]. Schematically speaking, MD5 is based on an "encryption function" e proposed by Davies-Meyer:

$$e : Z_2^{128} \times Z_2^{512} \to Z_2^{128}$$

then

$$e(K, L) = K + j(K, L)$$

where the addition is done in modulo 2^{32}.

The encryption $j(K, L)$ has four rounds and is described as follows:

- Message K has 128 bits and is arranged using a permutation (which depends on the round) into a word sequence, W_1, W_2, W_3, W_4

- Each of those words pass through sequential transformation, based on a Feistel scheme

- A transformation is defined by an S-box, where the input is (W_1, Key), the Key is derived from L, and the output is represented by W_2, W_3, W_4

- The output from the S-box is: ($A_1 + g_i(W_2, W_3, W_4) + Key + k_{i,j} + W_2) \lll \theta_{i,j}$, where $k_{i,j}$ and $\theta_{i,j}$ are defined as a table, and g_i represents a Boolean function round defined as follows:

$$g_1(W_2, W_3, W_4) = (W_2 \wedge W_3) \vee ((\neg W_2) \wedge W_4)$$

$$g_2(W_2, W_3, W_4) = (W_4 \wedge W_2) \vee ((\neg W_4) \wedge W_3)$$

$$g_3(W_2, W_3, W_4) = W_2 \oplus W_3 \oplus W_4$$

$$g_4(W_2, W_3, W_4) = W_3 \oplus (W_2 \wedge (\neg W_4))$$

SHA1 Function

SHA1 represents a variant of the SHA hash function, noted as standard FIPS 180-1, which was a correction of a small weakness in SHA.

Let's consider y ($|y| \leq 2^{64} - 1$), the binary string that needs to be hashed or marked. The first part of SHA1 is similar to the one from MD4 (see Algorithm 8-1).

If $|s| < 64$, zeroes are added to the left until it reaches an equality. The final block T (which enters in the hash algorithm) has a length that is divisible by 512. We will represent it as a concatenation of n blocks, each of the block with 512 bits:

$$T = T_1 \| T_2 \| \ldots \| T_n$$

Consider the following functions $g_e : Z_2^{32} \times Z_2^{32} \times Z_2^{32} \to Z_2^{32}$ $(0 \leq e \leq 79)$, defined as follows:

$$g_e = \{(W_2 \wedge W_3) \vee ((\neg B) \wedge W_4) \qquad 0 \leq e \leq 19 \, W_2 \oplus W_3 \oplus W_4$$
$$20 \leq e \leq 39 \, (W_2 \wedge W_3) \vee (W_2 \wedge W_4) \vee (W_3 \wedge W_4) \qquad 40 \leq e \leq 59 \, W_2 \oplus W_3 \oplus W_4$$
$$60 \leq e \leq 79$$

Each function g_e takes three words as input and outputs one word.

The next step is to define the following constants, C_0, C_1, ..., C_{79} as follows:

$$C_t = \{(5ab27999)_{16} \qquad 0 \leq t \leq 19 \, (6ed9eba1)_{16} \qquad 20 \leq t \leq 39$$
$$(8f1bbcdc)_{16} \qquad 40 \leq t \leq 59 \, (ca62c1d6)_{16} \qquad 60 \leq t \leq 79$$

The SHA1 compression algorithm is as follows:

1. $J_0 \leftarrow (67452301)_{16}$, $J_1 \leftarrow (efcdab89)_{16}$, $J_2 \leftarrow (98badcfe)_{16}$,

$$J_3 \leftarrow (10325476)_{16}, \; J_4 \leftarrow (c3d2e1f0)_{16}$$

2. *for* $i \leftarrow 1$ *to* n *do*

    a. Set $T_i = L_0 \| L_1 \| \ldots \| L_{15}, L_i \in Z_2^{32}$

    b. *for* $t \leftarrow 16$ *to* 79 *do*

        i. $L_i \leftarrow (L_t - 3 \oplus L_{t-8} \oplus L_{t-14} \oplus L_{t-16} \lll 1)$

   c. $W_1 \leftarrow L_0, \ W_2 \leftarrow L_1, \ W_3 \leftarrow L_2, W_4 \leftarrow L_3, W_5 \leftarrow L_4$

   d. *for* $t \leftarrow 0$ *to* 79 *do*

      i. *temp* $\leftarrow (W_1 \lll 5) + g_e(W_2, W_3, W_4) + E + L_T + C_t$

      ii. $W_5 \leftarrow W_4, W_4 \leftarrow W_3, W_3 \leftarrow (W_2 \lll 30), W_2 \leftarrow W_1$

      iii. $W_1 \leftarrow temp$

   e. $J_0 \leftarrow J_0 + W_1, \quad J_1 \leftarrow J_1 + W_2,$

$$J_2 \leftarrow J_2 + W_3, J_3 \leftarrow J_3 + W_4, J_4 \leftarrow J_4 + W_5$$

The SHA1 hash function generates a block of 160 bits for each block of 512 bits.

Implementing Hash Functions

There are two general ways to implement hash functions in MATLAB. The method used depends on multiple aspects, such as experience, how fast the implementation should be provided, the reason the implementation is done, how sensitive the software application is, whether the library has been tested for security breaches, and so on.

The first method uses third-party libraries and namespaces from other programming languages (e.g., Java), such as `java.security`. For this mode of implementation, we provided an example in Listing 8-3.

The second implementation method is the so-called *from scratch* implementation. This means that we are already familiar with the steps from the algorithms, and we will write the implementation of the hash function from scratch (see Listing 8-4).

The advantages of this implementation are based on the fact that we know what we have done, we are aware of the vulnerable points of the algorithms and what parts of the code can be exploited in order to corrupt the algorithm, and it's easy to customize once we have a full script (source code). The disadvantages are that it's time consuming and we need a good understanding of the MATLAB functions and the hash algorithms. See Figure 8-3.

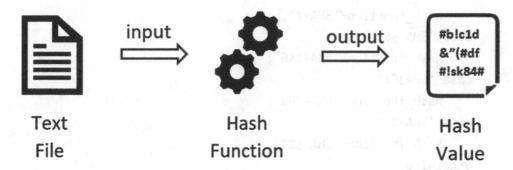

Figure 8-3. *Hash function workflow*

Implementing SHA-1/256/368/512, MD2, and MD5

This section shows the first way of implementation (using third-party libraries and namespaces), as it is more convenient for most of the developers, researchers, and specialists. Listing 8-3 shows a complex example using MATLAB and `java.security` to provide a general implementation of hash functions, such as SHA-1, SHA-256, SHA-368, SHA-512, as well as MD2 and MD5.

Let's suppose that we have a text message or file and we want to provide a digest value of it (or a hash value).

Listing 8-3. General Implementation for Different Hash Functions

```matlab
1    function my_hash_result = Listing83(data_input,hash_function)
2    data_input=data_input(:);
3    % the data input will be converted into an UINT8 format
4    if ischar(data_input) || islogical(data_input)
5        data_input=uint8(data_input);
6
7    % implemented for not having any losses of the input data
8    else
9        data_input=typecast(data_input,'uint8');
10   end
11
12   % verify hash method
13   hash_function=upper(hash_function);
14   switch hash_function
15       case 'SHA1'
```

```
16                hash_function='SHA-1';
17        case 'SHA256'
18                hash_function='SHA-256';
19        case 'SHA384'
20                hash_function='SHA-384';
21        case 'SHA512'
22                hash_function='SHA-512';
23        otherwise
24    end
25
26    al={'MD2','MD5','SHA-1','SHA-256','SHA-384','SHA-512'};
27    if isempty(strmatch(hash_function,al,'exact'))
28        error(['Hash algorithm must be ' ...
29            MD2, MD5, SHA-1, SHA-256, SHA-384, or SHA-512']);
30    end
31
32    % generate the hash using the mentioned algorithms
33    jhf=java.security.MessageDigest.getInstance(hash_function);
34    jhf.update(data_input);
35    my_hash_result=typecast(jhf.digest,'uint8');
36    my_hash_result=dec2hex(my_hash_result)';
37
38    % if it is the case that all hashes bytes are less than
39    % 128, then perform with a padding operation
40    if(size(my_hash_result,1))==1
41        my_hash_result=[repmat('0',[1
42    size(my_hash_result,2)]);my_hash_result];
43    end
44    my_hash_result=lower(my_hash_result(:)');
45    clear x
46    return
```

In Line 1, we declared the my_hash_result function, which receives two inputs, data_input and hash_function. data_input is the message we want to compute to a digest (hash value), using the algorithm specified in the hash_function parameter.

In Line 4 with ischar, we perform a test to see if the input is an array of characters and with islogical we determine if the input is a logical array. In Line 9 with typecast, we convert the input value to uint8, which will also work with uint16. In Line 13, we converted the name of the hash function to uppercase.

In Lines 14-24, we are determining with the switch instruction what type of hash function we specified as the input. In Line 26, we declare a unidimensional vector called al in which we specify all the hash functions and algorithms that we are using. With the strmatch function, we are determining if the hash function provided as the input matches exactly (see the exact keyword) the elements of the vector al. Once the result is obtained, we use isempty to see if we have elements or not. If we specify other algorithms that are not found in the vector, the error in Line 28 is thrown.

In Line 32, the getInstance method initializes the variable x with the algorithm specified and holds hash_function as input. The getInstance method is from the java. security package, and it provides a certain level of power and confidence in the process of hashing the inputs. In Line 34, we update the settings properly with the input. In Line 35, we compute the digest (the hash value) for jhf with the digest method, and secondly, we make sure that it's converted to uint8 using the typecast method. Note in Lines 32 and 34 that jhf has the hash algorithm and the input. In Line 36, we convert the hash result from decimal to hexadecimal using the hex2dec method.

Between Lines 40 and 43, we perform the padding operation if all the hash's lengths are less than 128. In Line 40, with the help of the size function, we return the size of the first element from my_hash_result, and determine if it's equal to 1. In Line 41, the padding operation is performed. The repmat function is used to repeat a copy of the array, and it shows how the items of the array are arranged.

In Line 44, the result is converted to lowercase and shown in the Command Window. In Line 45, we clear the workspace and the memory of x.

Figure 8-4 shows the result of an explicit example of input. To run the script in Listing 8-1, open MATLAB. Make sure that your script is open properly and the path has been added accordingly, then type the following function call:

```
my_hash_result=Listing83Listing81('Welcome to Apress', 'SHA512')
```

Figure 8-4. *The output for a specific hash algorithm*

In Listing 8-4, we provided an example that computes multiple hash values on the same input using the algorithms specified in the hash_algorithms array.

In Line 1, we declare an array, hash_algorithms, which stores the name of the hash algorithms as its elements. In Line 11, we compute the hash value for each of the hash algorithms n Line 1 by invoking the function in Listing 8-3, and we show the result in the Command Window (see Figure 8-5). Lines 4 to 9 show the general messages that are shown in the Command Window.

Listing 8-4. Computing Hash Values Using Multiple Hash Algorithms for an Input

```
1   hash_algorithms={'MD2','MD5','SHA-1','SHA-256','SHA-
2   384','SHA-512'};
3
4   disp('Welcome to Apress!');
5   disp('------------------');
6   disp('The following text will be hashed using the hash
7   algorithms from below');
8   disp('The text is: Good luck with Hash Functions!');
9   disp(' ');
10
11  for n=1:6
12      my_hash_result = Listing83('Good luck with Hash
13  Functions!',hash_algorithms{n});
14      disp([hash_algorithms{n} ' ('
15  num2str(length(my_hash_result)*4) ' bits):'])
16      disp(my_hash_result)
17  end
```

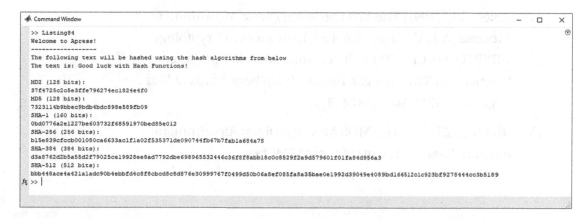

Figure 8-5. *Computing hash values on the same input with different algorithms*

Conclusion

This chapter presented the basic hash functions, including MD4, MD5, and SHA1, serving as a main guideline for providing the proper implementations for the next algorithms.

An implementation in MATLAB was provided for computing hash values using the SHA1, SHA256, SHA384, SHA512, MD2, and MD5 hash algorithms.

References

[1]   Canuto, Claudio, and Anita Tabacco. *Mathematical Analysis I.* Springer International Publishing, 2015. *DOI.org (Crossref),* doi:10.1007/978-3-319-12772-9.

[2]   Mihailescu, Marius Iulian, and Stefania Loredana Nita. *Pro Cryptography and Cryptanalysis: Creating Advanced Algorithms with C# and .NET.* Apress, 2021. *DOI.org (Crossref),* doi:10.1007/978-1-4842-6367-9.

[3]   Mihailescu, Marius Iulian, and Stefania Loredana Nita. *Pro Cryptography and Cryptanalysis with C++20: Creating and Programming Advanced Algorithms.* Apress, 2021. DOI.org (Crossref), doi:10.1007/978-1-4842-6586-4.

[4]   Rivest R.L. (1991) The MD4 Message Digest Algorithm. In: Menezes A.J., Vanstone S.A. (eds) Advances in Cryptology-CRYPTO' 90. CRYPTO 1990. Lecture Notes in Computer Science, vol 537. Springer, Berlin, Heidelberg. `https://doi.org/10.1007/3-540-38424-3_22`.

[5]   Rivest R.L. (1992) The MD5 Message Digest Algorithm. In: `https://www.ietf.org/rfc/rfc1321.txt`

CHAPTER 9

Block Ciphers: DES and AES

This chapter discusses block ciphers, such as the *Data Encryption System* (DES) and the *Advanced Encryption System* (AES). Different aspects, such as substitution/permutation, are discussed as design techniques used with block ciphers. This approach is based on FIPS 46-3 for DES and FIPS-197 for AES.

An important aspect to be noted is the fact that DES was withdrawn on May 19, 2005. A historical list of the reasons can be consulted in [1]. The DES algorithm is not used anymore and, in this section, we treat it as a model of implementation for other block ciphers or with the purpose of designing and implementing practical solutions.

Preliminaries

The designing process of the block ciphers is based on two main components: the *iterated cipher* and *substitution operations* [2].

The *iterated cipher* is based on the *round function* and on the *key schedule*. The message encryption process goes through a set of M rounds.

According to [2], let's proceed further with the process of constructing the *key schedule* from K, where $K = \{K_1, ..., K_M\}$ is the set of *round keys* or *subkeys*. This is achieved using a fixed, public algorithm.

The next step defines a round function, called r_f, which receives as inputs two parameters: the round key K_r and a current state, denoted as q^{r-1}. Based on the notation set for the state, the next state is computed as $q^r = r_f(q^{r-1}, K_r)$. The q_0 state is the initial

© Marius Iulian Mihailescu and Stefania Loredana Nita 2021
M. I. Mihailescu and S. L. Nita, *Cryptography and Cryptanalysis in MATLAB*,
https://doi.org/10.1007/978-1-4842-7334-0_9

state and represents the message, m. The encrypted version of the message is denoted with c and is obtained once all M rounds are computed. As an example, the encryption process will look like [2]:

$$q_0 \leftarrow m$$

$$q_1 \leftarrow r_f(q_0, K_1)$$

$$q_2 \leftarrow r_f(q_1, K_2)$$

$$\vdots \quad \vdots \quad \vdots \quad \vdots \quad \vdots \quad \vdots$$

$$q_{M-1} \leftarrow r_f(q_{M-2}, K_{M-1})$$

$$q_N \leftarrow r_f(q_{M-1}, K_N)$$

$$c \leftarrow q_N$$

The decryption process is the inverse of the encryption, and for this to be done properly, the function r_f has to satisfy some properties. One of them is to be injective if the second parameter is fixed. In simple words, this means that there is a function r_f^{-1} that satisfies the following property:

$$r_f^{-1}(r_f(q, c), c) = q, \forall q, c$$

At this point, we can compute the decryption function [2]:

$$q_M \leftarrow c$$

$$q_{M-1} \leftarrow r_f^{-1}(q_M, K_M)$$

$$\vdots \quad \vdots \quad \vdots \quad \vdots \quad \vdots \quad \vdots$$

$$q_1 \leftarrow r_f^{-1}(q_2, K_2)$$

$$q_0 \leftarrow r_f^{-1}(q_1, K_1)$$

$$m \leftarrow q_0$$

Networks Based on Substitution and Permutation

In the modern process of designing block ciphers, substitution and permutation networking play an important role. A network based on substitution and/or permutation is a new approach and a special type of iterated cipher [2].

The goal of this subsection is to explain the theoretical operations of networks based on substitution and permutation, as they are vital once we get to the implementation. They play an important role in implementing block ciphers (e.g., DES).

Suppose that we have we positive integers, a and b. Once we have a message/plaintext (m) and an encrypted version of the message, their representation will occur as binary arrays and their length will be the product of the two positive integers, a and b. The product $a \cdot b$ is the *length of the block*.

Such a network is designed with respect to two components, noted as φ_{Sbox} and φ_p, and defined as follows: $\varphi_{Sbox} : \{0,1\}^a \to \{0,1\}^a$. This permutation has a length (a) of 2^a bitstrings, and $\varphi_p : \{1, ... a \cdot b\} \to \{1, ..., a \cdot b\}$ is a permutation as well, with integers $1, ..., a \cdot m$. The first permutation defined as φ_{Sbox} is an *S-box* and its purpose is to replace the a bits with a different set of a bits. The second permutation φ_p has a secondary purpose, defined as the permutation process of $a \cdot b$ bits by changing the order of those bits.

Say we have a binary string with $a \cdot b$-bit length. We will consider $u = (u_1, ..., u_{a \cdot b})$ as the concatenation of the substrings from $a \cdot b$-bit, denoted as $u_{<1>}, ..., u_{<m>}$. That being said, the following expression is true: $u = u_{<1>} \| ... \| u_{<m>}$. For the following inequalities $1 \leq i \leq a$, the following expression exists as well: $u_{<i>} = (u_{(i-1) \cdot a + 1}, ..., u_{i \cdot a})$.

The networks are based on T rounds. Within each round, we compute a substitutions based on φ_{Sbox}. A computation for permutation φ_p is also performed. Cryptosystem 9-1 can be found in [2].

Cryptosystem 9-1. Network Based on Substitution-Permutation

"Consider a, b, and T positive integers. We will
note with $\varphi_{Sbox} : \{0,1\}^a \to \{0,1\}^a$ the permutation and
$\varphi_p : \{1, ..., a \cdot b\} \to \{1, ..., a \cdot b\}$ another permutation. Consider that
$P = C = \{0,1\}^{a \cdot b}$, and $K \subseteq (\{0,1\}^{a \cdot b})^{T+1}$ to be all the possible key
schedules that are derived from an initial key K based on the algorithm
used for scheduling algorithm. Using the key schedule $(K_1, ..., K_{T+1})$, the
encryption process for the plaintext is provided by Algorithm 9-1." [2]

In Algorithm 9-1, $input_r$ is the input for the s-boxes at round r, and $output_r$ is represented by the output from the s-boxes in round r. Next, $output_r'$ is obtained from $output_r$ by applying the permutation φ_{Sbox}. Following the nature of the algorithm, $input_{r+1}$ is constructed using $output_r$ with the help of an XOR operation and with the round key ξr^{+1}. This process is known as *round key mixing*. As we will observe in the algorithm and as well as in the implementation of DES or AES, the permutation φ_{Sbox} is not applied in the last round.

Algorithm 9-1. NETWORK($msg, \varphi_{Sbox}, \varphi_p, (K_1, ..., K_{T+1})$) [2]

$$q_0 \leftarrow msg$$

$$for \; round \leftarrow 1 \, to \, T - 1$$

$$do\{input_{round} \leftarrow q^{round-1} \oplus K^{round} \; for \, i \leftarrow 1 \, to \, msg \, do \, output_{\langle i \rangle}^{round}$$

$$\leftarrow \varphi_{Sbox}\left(input_{\langle i \rangle}^{round}\right) q_{round} \leftarrow (output_{\varphi_p(1)}^{round}, ..., output_{\varphi_p(a \cdot b)}^{round}$$

$$input^T \leftarrow q^{T-1} \oplus K^{round}$$

$$for \; i \leftarrow 1 \, to \, msg$$

$$do \, output_{\langle i \rangle}^T \leftarrow \varphi_{Sbox}\left(input_{\langle i \rangle}^T\right)$$

$$c \leftarrow output^T \oplus K^{T+1}$$

$$output(c)$$

Attacks Based on Linear Cryptanalysis

This section introduces some references that will help you design and implement such attacks.

The main goal of linear cryptanalysis is to find or to determine a probabilistic linear relationship between a subset of bits (from the message) and another subset formed from the state bits that precede the substitutions computed in the last round.

In order to achieve a linear cryptanalysis, you must provide a flexible justification involved in the attack. We must also create an overview of the results represented by the probability theory.

When designing and preparing to implement such attacks in MATLAB, we need to have a deep understanding of the main theoretical aspects from probability theory and a strong knowledge of programming with MATLAB and C++. [5] and [6] have dedicated chapters on how to implement linear cryptanalysis for DES in C++20 and C#. Most of the C++20 examples can be adjusted to work within MATLAB scripts. A very interesting linear attack can be seen in [2] and a couple of examples of practical attacks are in [6].

The main tools from the probability theory are in the *Piling-up Lemma* [2, 10-14] and *Linear Approximations of S-boxes* [15-17]. We will not go through the mathematical background of the probability tools at this point, due to their complexity. It's a good idea to consult the resources before proceeding with the MATLAB implementations.

Attacks Based on Differential Cryptanalysis

Differential cryptanalysis has multiple similarities with linear cryptanalysis. One of the main differences with linear cryptanalysis is that, in differential cryptanalysis, we compare XOR operations from two inputs (*j*) with their corresponding two outputs.

The purpose of this section is not to provide the entire mathematical background. To understanding the main theoretical concepts, you are strongly encouraged to follow the resources: [2], [4], [5], [6], and [14] – [17]. These resources explain the concepts that are necessary to implement attacks based on differential cryptanalysis.

Differential cryptanalysis focuses on the inputs, i and i^*, which are binary strings with a fixed $i - or$ value, noted by the following relation $i' = y \oplus Y^*$.

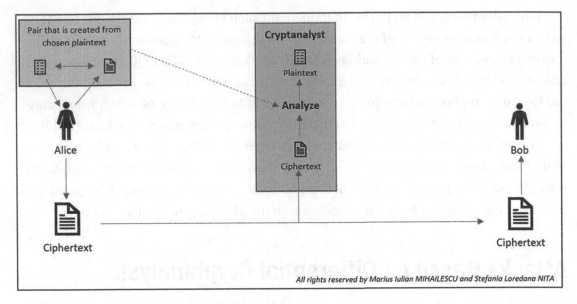

Figure 9-1. *Chosen-plaintext attack (CPA)*

Differential cryptanalysis is based on a chosen-plaintext attack (see Figure 9-1). We start from the assumption that an attacker generates a large number of tuples (j, j^*, i, i^*), where i or value $i' = i \oplus i^*$ is fixed. The encryption process is based on the same unknown key, K, having the same encrypted strings j and j^*. For each of the tuples, the decryption is applied on the ciphertexts j and j^*.

When we use a CPA, the cryptanalyst can pick the plaintext that was encrypted and sent using an encryption algorithm (e.g., DES) and can observe the entire process of how the ciphertext is generated. Everything that is observed can be treated as an active model in which the cryptanalyst can pick the plaintext and perform the encryption. Using this opportunity based on selecting and pick plaintext, the attacker or the cryptanalysis can work on important details with respect to the ciphertext. Once the cryptanalyst gets inside of the "mystery box," they can get to the secret key. Most attackers and professional cryptanalysts will have their own databases that store known plaintexts, ciphertexts, and possible encryption keys [6].

The Data Encryption Standard (DES)

The story behind DES is very interesting and starts on May 15, 1973, when the National Bureau of Standards (now known as the National Institute of Standards and Technology, NIST) launched a solicitation for cryptosystems in the Federal Register [2]. DES was adopted and shortly became well known in the world. DES was developed by IBM based on the Lucifer algorithm, a previous algorithm, and was first published on March 17, 1975.

DES Description

One of the most comprehensive descriptions of DES is provided in the Federal Information Processing Standards (FIPS) publication 46 from January 15, 1977. It is very important to note that DES is based on a Feistel network, known as a Feistel cipher as well. Let's take a quick look at the Feistel cipher.

Starting from a Feistel cipher, the states s^i are divided into two equal chunks of the same length, denoted as X^i and Y^i. The found function r_f has the following form: $r_f(X^{i-1}, Y^{i-1}, K^i) = (X^i, Y^i)$, where X^i and Y^i are defined as follows:

$$X^i = Y^{i-1}$$

$$Y^i = X^{i-1} \oplus v\left(X^{i-1}, K^i\right).$$

Once we reach this point, we can observe that function v will not satisfy the injective property. This is because the Feistel-type round function is always invertible, based on the round key:

$$X^{i-1} = Y^i \oplus v\left(Y^i, K^i\right)$$

$$Y^{i-1} = X^i.$$

DES is characterized as a Feistel cipher round of 16 bits with a block that has 64 bits. The message is encrypted as a bitstring m with a length of 64 bits, and the encryption key is 56 bits long. The encrypted message has the same length, 64 bits. In total we have a set of 16 rounds, and a fixed initial permutation (IP) is applied to the message (plaintext). The following notation is available:

$$IP(m) = X^0 Y^0.$$

Once we get to the end of the set of rounds, the inverse permutation is used over the bitstring $X^{16}Y^{16}$, obtaining the ciphertext c, as follows:

$$c = IP^{-1}\left(X^{16}, Y^{16}\right).$$

From the cryptographic point of view, *IP* and *IP*$^{-1}$ do not have significance, and sometimes they are ignored when security of DES is discussed.

Starting from the fact that X^i and Y^i are 32 bits long, the function is available and recommended to be used during the implementation:

$$f : \{0,1\}^{32} \times \{0,1\}^{48} \to \{0,1\}^{32}$$

The function *f* will take as input a 32-bit long string and the key (e.g., round key). As we saw in the mathematical properties, the key schedule $(K^1, K^2, ..., K^{16})$ is based on a round key of 48 bits and are derived from a key of 56 bits.

We strongly advise you to get familiarized with the entire mathematical background and to go deeply for a complete understanding of the entire mechanisms behind DES, such as references [2] and [4].

Implementation of DES

Moving forward to the true purpose of the chapter, Listing 9-1 shows an implementation in MATLAB.

At this moment we will generate the encryption key (see Listing 9-1). It will generate 8 × 8 vector (array) DES keys by default that have the parity check bits (see Line 5) and a random binary block of 64 bits for IV as the initialization vector. An important aspect is allocating space and randomly generating a binary block that's 8 × 7 in size (see Line 4). The output is in a binary matrix, as shown in Figure 9-2. To run the script, just type the following in the Command Window: *key* = *Listing*91. The variable *key* will store the binary matrix that we will use in Listing91 to encrypt or decrypt messages.

Listing 9-1. Key Generation Script

```
1    function cryptography_key=Listing91(a,b)
2    switch nargin
3        case 0
4            cryptography_key=round(rand(8,7));
5            cryptography_key(:,8)=
6    mod(sum(cryptography_key,2)+1,2);
7        case 1
8            cryptography_key=cell(1,a);
9            for i=1:a
```

```
10              key=round(rand(8,7));
11              key(:,8)= mod(sum(key,2)+1,2);
12              cryptography_key{i}=key;
13          end
14      case 2
15          if a>1
16              cryptography_key=cell(2,b);
17          else
18              cryptography_key=cell(1,b);
19          end
20          for j=1:m
21              key= round(rand(8,7));
22              key(:,8)= mod(sum(key,2)+1,2);
23              cryptography_key{1,j}=key;
24              if a > 1
25                  cryptography_key{2,j}=round(rand(8,8));
26              end
27          end
28  end
29  assignin('base','GENERATE_CRYPTO_KEY',cryptography_key)
```

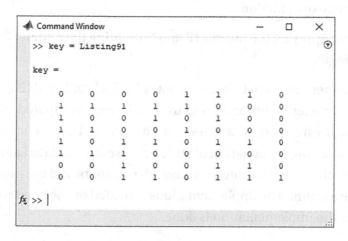

Figure 9-2. *The key generation script output*

For encryption and decryption operations, one of the best ways to provide a proper implementation in MATLAB is to use the ECB mode. It is easy, fast, and reliable, and you can adjust it quickly for the other modes. The implementation follows some basic phases, called *sections*. These sections are straightforward and standardized due to the fact that the NIST standard[1] has to be followed properly.

A proper implementation has five sections:

- *Section 1: Parity Validation.* Each block of 8 bits needs to have an odd number that has ones.

- *Section 2: The Key Schedule.* In this section we provide a functionality that will split and permute the key using the parity validation 1. A very important aspect is that the bits from the parity validation are ignored.

- *Section 3: The initial Permutation (IP) and Inverse IP.* The section has two main operations, the permutation before the main rounds of cipher of the block that is the plaintext block, and the permutation of the block for the output that is done with inverse IP.

- *Section 4: Generation of Feistel Network.* The IP has to be divided into two chunks, a left and right. We also provided a permutation for expansion and s-boxes, including applying the 16 rounds from the Feistel network function.

- *Section 5:* Applying the inverse IP and formatting the output accordingly.

The best implementations of DES can be found at [24], [25], and [26]. The implementations were tested properly, and the results were compared with authorized and well-known software, such as CrypTool[2] or Kali Linux[3]. There is no point at this moment to provide an implementation of DES, because it is outdated and not secure anymore, and the references indicated are enough to understand the main concepts behind the DES algorithm. The implementations provided by the cited references can be used to study how the implementation is done.

---

[1] SP 800-17: https://csrc.nist.gov/publications/detail/sp/800-17/archive/1998-02-01
[2] https://www.cryptool.org
[3] https://tools.kali.org/tools-listing

As an example, consider the similar outputs in Figure 9-3 and Figure 9-4. The examples were obtained from reference [24].

```
Encryption('welcome to cryptography', key, 'ENC')
Decryption('encrypted value', key, 'DEC')
```

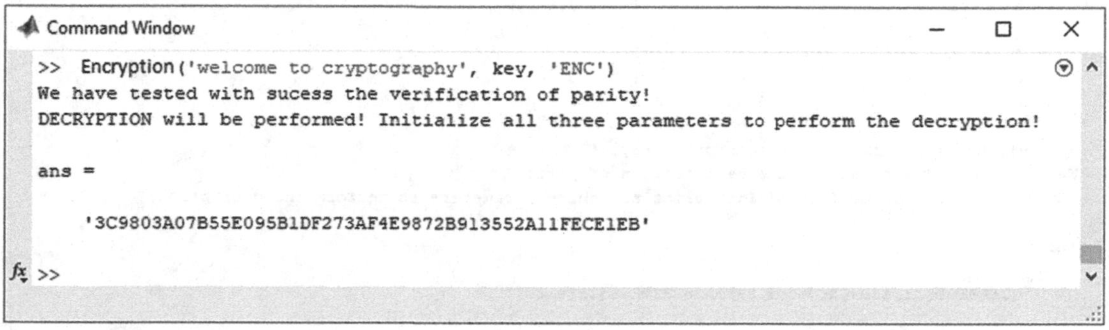

Figure 9-3. *DES encryption output*

Figure 9-4. *DES decryption output*

The whole DES process of generating the key, encryption, and decryption is shown in Figure 9-5.

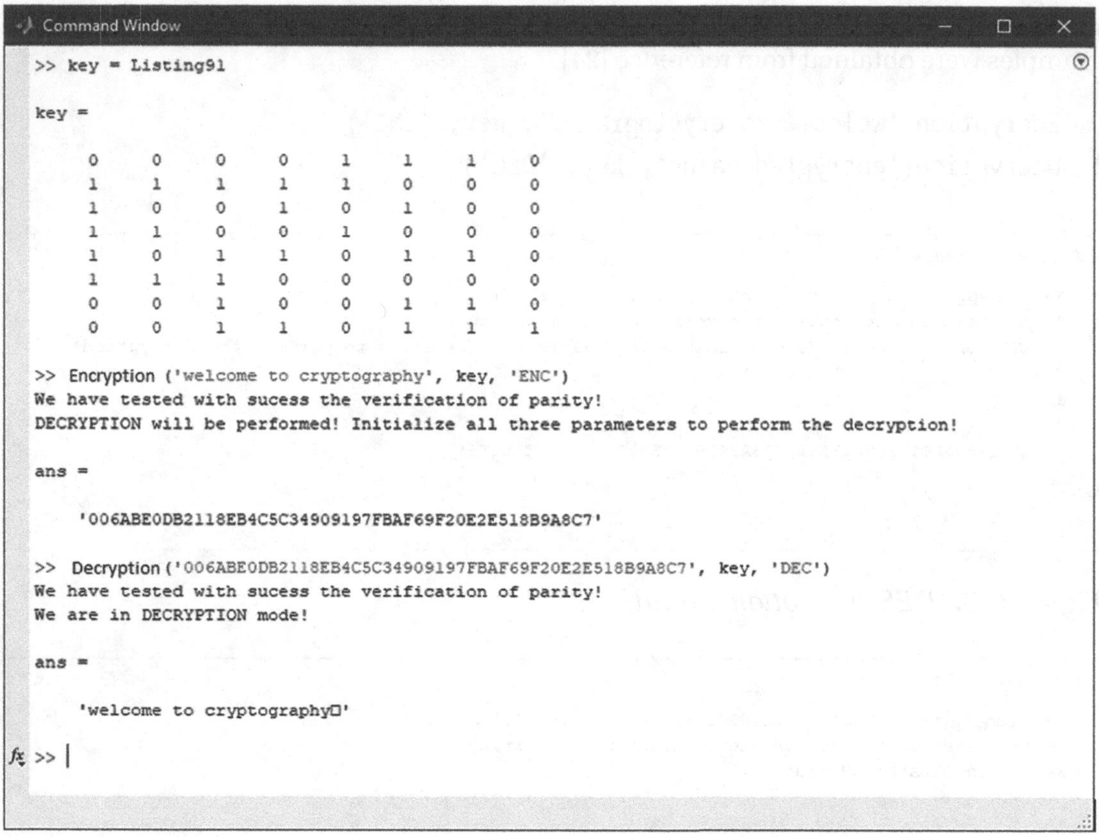

```
Command Window                                                    —   □   ×

>> key = Listing91

key =

      0    0    0    0    1    1    1    0
      1    1    1    1    1    0    0    0
      1    0    0    1    0    1    0    0
      1    1    0    0    1    0    0    0
      1    0    1    1    0    1    1    0
      1    1    1    0    0    0    0    0
      0    0    1    0    0    1    1    0
      0    0    1    1    0    1    1    1

>> Encryption ('welcome to cryptography', key, 'ENC')
We have tested with sucess the verification of parity!
DECRYPTION will be performed! Initialize all three parameters to perform the decryption!

ans =

    '006ABE0DB2118EB4C5C34909197FBAF69F20E2E518B9A8C7'

>> Decryption ('006ABE0DB2118EB4C5C34909197FBAF69F20E2E518B9A8C7', key, 'DEC')
We have tested with sucess the verification of parity!
We are in DECRYPTION mode!

ans =

    'welcome to cryptography□'

fx >> |
```

Figure 9-5. *The entire process of generating the key, encryption, and decryption for DES*

The Advanced Encryption System (AES)

The Advanced Encryption Standard (AES) is a symmetric encryption scheme, the successor of the DES encryption scheme. In 1997, NIST launched a competition to elect an AES that would replace DES. In 2001, NIST announced the winner cryptosystem, which was a block cipher proposed by the Belgian cryptographers Vincent Rijmen and Joan Daemen. Their proposal was based on the Rijndael block cipher. The standards that describe AES are FIPS PUB 197: Advanced Encryption Standard (AES) [18] and ISO/IEC 18033-3: Block ciphers [19].

AES uses iterations and the number of rounds, denoted with , is different in relation to the length of the secret key, which is denoted with l_{sk}^{AES}. The lengths of the AES cipher are as follows:

- The length of the block: 128 bits

- Possible lengths for the key: 128, 192, or 256 bits

These being said, the number of rounds can be if $l_{sk}^{AES} = 128$ then $n = 10$, if $l_{sk}^{AES} = 192$ then $n = 12$, or if $l_{sk}^{AES} = 256$ then $n = 14$.

To encrypt a plain message x using AES, the following steps should be followed [1]:

- *State* is initialized with x, then the AddRoundKey operation is executed. Here, AddRoundKey applies an *XOR* operation between *RoundKey* and *State*.

- The SubBytes operation is executed for the first $n - 1$ rounds, then the ShiftRows permutation is executed, followed by the MixColumn operation, and finally, the AddRoundKey operation is executed. Here, the operations work as follows:

- SubBytes is applied on *State* based on an *S-box*.

- ShiftRows is applied on *State*.

- MixColumn is applied on *State*.

- In the last round, the following operations are executed again: SubBytes, ShiftRows, and AddRoundKey.

- The encrypted message is $y = State$.

Further, we describe the operations used in AES, both for encryption and decryption, as they are included in the standard [18]. Additional examples are found in [2] and [20].

Before continuing, note that the operations in AES are applied to bytes, and the parameters used are represented on a specific number of bytes. The plain message x is represented in 16 bytes, let's denote them $x_0, \dots, x_{15}$, while *State* is organized as a $4x4$ matrix of bytes, which is initialized with the values of x, as follows:

$$\left[s_{0,0}\ s_{0,1}\ s_{0,2}\ s_{0,3}\ s_{1,0}\ s_{1,1}\ s_{1,2}\ s_{1,3}\ s_{2,0}\ s_{2,1}\ s_{2,2}\ s_{2,3}\ s_{3,0}\ s_{3,1}\ s_{3,2}\ s_{3,3} \right]$$
$$\equiv \left[x_0\ x_4\ x_8\ x_{12}\ x_1\ x_5\ x_9\ x_{13}\ x_2\ x_6\ x_{10}\ x_{14}\ x_3\ x_7\ x_{11}\ x_{15} \right]$$

For convenience, the representation of a byte will utilize the hexadecimal notation, which leads to a representation of two hexadecimal digits.

SubBytes Operations

The purpose of this operation is to separately substitute every byte contained in *State* based on an S-box, called π_S. In fact, π_S is a permutation of the set $\{0, 1\}^8$, for whose representation the hexadecimal notation is used. Table 9-1 shows the AES S-box.

Table 9-1. *AES S-Box*

X	Y															
	0	1	2	3	4	5	6	7	8	9	A	B	C	D	E	F
0	63	7C	77	7B	F2	6B	6F	C5	30	01	67	2B	FE	D7	AB	76
1	CA	82	C9	7D	FA	59	47	F0	AD	D4	A2	AF	9C	A4	72	C0
2	B7	FD	93	26	36	3F	F7	CC	34	A5	E5	F1	71	D8	31	15
3	04	C7	23	C3	18	96	05	9A	07	12	80	E2	EB	27	B2	75
4	09	83	2C	1A	1B	6E	5A	A0	52	3B	D6	B3	29	E3	2F	84
5	53	D1	00	ED	20	FC	B1	5B	6A	CB	BE	39	4A	4C	58	CF
6	D0	EF	AA	FB	43	4D	33	85	45	F9	02	7F	50	3C	9F	A8
7	51	A3	40	8F	92	9D	38	F5	BC	B6	DA	21	10	FF	F3	D2
8	CD	0C	13	EC	5F	97	44	17	C4	A7	7E	3D	64	5D	19	73
9	60	81	4F	DC	22	2A	90	88	46	EE	B8	14	DE	5E	0B	DB
A	E0	32	3A	0A	49	06	24	5C	C2	D3	AC	62	91	95	E4	79
B	E7	C8	37	6D	8D	D5	4E	A9	6C	56	F4	EA	65	7A	AE	08
C	BA	78	25	2E	1C	A6	B4	C6	E8	DD	74	1F	4B	BD	8B	8A
D	70	3E	B5	66	48	03	F6	0E	61	35	57	B9	86	C1	1D	9E
E	E1	F8	98	11	69	D9	8E	94	9B	1E	87	E9	CE	55	28	DF
F	8C	A1	89	0D	BF	E6	42	68	41	99	2D	0F	B0	54	BB	16

The rows are denoted with X and the columns with Y, and a specific value is referred as $\pi_S(XY)$. To construct the S-box, algebraic operations are applied in the finite field:

$$GF\left(2^8\right) = Z_2[x]/\left(x^8 + x^4 + x^3 + x + 1\right).$$

You can find the inverse of an element regarding the multiplication operation, convert a byte to an element of the field, and convert an element of the field to a byte.

The values in Table 9-1 were obtained using the following rules:

1. Compute the inverse of the element in $GF(2^8)$ regarding the multiplication operation. If the element is {00}, then the corresponding value is {00}, where the { } is a hexadecimal number.

2. Compute the affine transformation in $GF(2)$, for each $0 \leq i < 8$:

$$b_i' = b_i \oplus b_{(i+4)mod8} \oplus b_{(i+5)mod8} \oplus b_{(i+6)mod8} \oplus b_{(i+7)mod8} \oplus c_i,$$

where b_i represents the ith bit of the current byte, and c_i represents the ith bit of the byte $c = \{63\} \equiv \{01100011\}$. With the prime accent to the right, all variables are transformed with operations to the right.

The ShiftRows Operation

The purpose of this operation is to transform *State* by shifting the rows using the following rule:

$$\begin{bmatrix} s_{0,0}\ s_{0,1}\ s_{0,2}\ s_{0,3}\ s_{1,0}\ s_{1,1}\ s_{1,2}\ s_{1,3}\ s_{2,0}\ s_{2,1}\ s_{2,2}\ s_{2,3}\ s_{3,0}\ s_{3,1}\ s_{3,2}\ s_{3,3} \end{bmatrix}$$
$$shift \rightarrow \begin{bmatrix} s_{0,0}\ s_{0,1}\ s_{0,2}\ s_{0,3}\ s_{1,1}\ s_{1,2}\ s_{1,3}\ s_{1,0}\ s_{2,2}\ s_{2,3}\ s_{2,0}\ s_{2,1}\ s_{3,3}\ s_{3,0}\ s_{3,1}\ s_{3,2} \end{bmatrix}$$

The MixColumn Operation

The purpose of this operation is to replace the columns of *State*, following specific rules for each column. For the current column of *State* that is processed, the new column is the result of the multiplication between the current column and a particular matrix with elements chosen in $GF(2^8)$. The multiplication operation is the one from the field $GF(2^8)$. The two elements are used in the XOR operation that's applied to the bit strings corresponding to the two elements. That is because the addition between two elements of $GF(2^8)$ is the addition of components modulo 2. The AES states that each column is multiplied by a polynomial $a(x)$ given here, and then modulo $x^4 + 1$ is applied to the result:

$$a(x) = \{03\}x^3 + \{01\}x^2 + \{01\}x + \{02\}$$

In term of matrixes, *State* is obtained using the following matrix multiplication:

$$\left[\{02\} \{03\} \{01\} \{01\} \{01\} \{02\} \{03\} \{01\} \{01\} \{01\} \{02\} \{03\} \{03\} \{01\} \{01\} \{02\} \right]$$

$$\left[s_{0,0} \; s_{0,1} \; s_{0,2} \; s_{0,3} \; s_{1,0} \; s_{1,1} \; s_{1,2} \; s_{1,3} \; s_{2,0} \; s_{2,1} \; s_{2,2} \; s_{2,3} \; s_{3,0} \; s_{3,1} \; s_{3,2} \; s_{3,3} \right]$$

$$= \left[s'_{0,0} \; s'_{0,1} \; s'_{0,2} \; s'_{0,3} \; s'_{1,0} \; s'_{1,1} \; s'_{1,2} \; s'_{1,3} \; s'_{2,0} \; s'_{2,1} \; s'_{2,2} \; s'_{2,3} \; s'_{3,0} \; s'_{3,1} \; s'_{3,2} \; s'_{3,3} \right]$$

As an example, for the *i*th column of *State*, the elements are obtained as follows:

$$s'_{0,i} = \left(\{02\} \cdot s_{0,i} \right) \oplus \left(\{03\} \cdot s_{1,i} \right) \oplus s_{2,i} \oplus s_{3,i}$$

$$s'_{1,i} = s_{0,i} \oplus \left(\{02\} \cdot s_{1,i} \right) \oplus \left(\{03\} \cdot s_{2,i} \right) \oplus s_{3,i}$$

$$s'_{2,i} = s_{0,i} \oplus s_{1,i} \oplus \left(\{02\} \cdot s_{2,i} \right) \oplus \left(\{03\} \cdot s_{3,i} \right)$$

$$s'_{3,i} = \left(\{03\} \cdot s_{0,i} \right) \oplus s_{1,i} \oplus s_{2,i} \oplus \left(2 \cdot s_{3,i} \right)$$

In these equations, $\cdot$ represents the multiplication between the two elements of the field, and $\oplus$ represents the XOR operation between the bit strings.

The AddRoundKey Operation

The purpose of this operation is to add the key of the current round to *State*. This is accomplished by applying the XOR operation bitwise to the round key and *State*. The round key is a tuple of a number of words (called n_w) defined in the key schedule. Thus, each column of *State* is transformed following this rule:

$$\left[s'_{0,i}, s'_{1,i}, s'_{2,i}, s'_{3,i} \right] = \left[s_{0,i}, s_{1,i}, s_{2,i}, s_{3,i} \right] \oplus \left[w_{r*n_w+i} \right],$$

where $0 \leq i \leq n_w$, $0 \leq r \leq n_w$ and $[w_j]$ is a key schedule word.

Key Expansion

On each round, the encryption key is expanded with a certain number of words. Overall, the expansion is with a number of $n(n_w + 1)$ words, requiring an initial set of *nw* words. After the expansion, the new key is an array of words represented in four bytes.

To expand the key, two operations are used: SubWord and RotWord. The SubWord operation is executed on an input word represented on four bytes and transforms it by applying the S-box to every byte in the representation, resulting in an output word.

On the other hand, RotWord takes as its input the array $[a_0, a_1, a_2, a_3]$, on which it permutes cyclically yielding to the output $[a_1, a_2, a_3, a_0]$. The array of the current round consists of the tuple of values $[x^{i-1}, \{00\}, \{00\}, \{00\}]$, where x^{i-1} is a power of x applied in $GF(2^8)$.

To decrypt the message, the inverse operation is executed, namely InvSubBytes, InvShiftRows, InvMixColumn, and AddRoundKey.

InvSubBytes Operation

This operation is the inverse of SubBytes. It applies the inverse S-box to every bite of *State*. To obtain the inverse S-box, the inverse of the affine transformation used in SubBytes is computed and the inverse regarding the multiplication in $GF(2^8)$ is computed. The resulting inverse S-box is represented in Table 9-1.

InvShiftRows Operation

This operation is the inverse of the ShiftRows operation. It takes the *State* as input and shifts in the inverse direction the last three rows of *State*. It uses a circular shift on the right and one byte on the second to last row.

InvMixColumns Operation

This is the inverse of the MixColumns operation, and it is applied to each column of *State*. Here, the polynomial is $a^{-1}(x)$, with the following representation:

$$a^{-1}(x) = \{0b\}x^3 + \{od\}x^2 + \{09\}x + \{0e\},$$

with the same specifications as in MixColumns.
Therefore, the computations become:

$$\begin{bmatrix} \{0E\} \ \{0B\} \ \{0D\} \ \{09\} \ \{09\} \ \{0E\} \ \{0B\} \ \{0D\} \ \{0D\} \ \{09\} \ \{0E\} \ \{0B\} \ \{0B\} \ \{0D\} \ \{09\} \ \{0E\} \end{bmatrix}$$

$$\begin{bmatrix} s_{0,0} \ s_{0,1} \ s_{0,2} \ s_{0,3} \ s_{1,0} \ s_{1,1} \ s_{1,2} \ s_{1,3} \ s_{2,0} \ s_{2,1} \ s_{2,2} \ s_{2,3} \ s_{3_0} \ s_{3,1} \ s_{3,2} \ s_{3,3} \end{bmatrix}$$

$$= \begin{bmatrix} s'_{0,0} \ s'_{0,1} \ s'_{0,2} \ s'_{0,3} \ s'_{1,0} \ s'_{1,1} \ s'_{1,2} \ s'_{1,3} \ s'_{2,0} \ s'_{2,1} \ s'_{2,2} \ s'_{2,3} \ s'_{3,0} \ s'_{3,1} \ s'_{3,2} \ s'_{3,3} \end{bmatrix}$$

The AES encryption system is widely implemented in different programming languages. There are several implementations in MATLAB that we tested and that work properly. Some of them can be found in [21] and [22].

The AES encryption system is in theory unbreakable if it is implemented correctly. One of the vulnerable parts that should be taken into consideration is the secret key used for encryption and decryption—it needs to be encrypted in order to be protected.

One type of attack that can break AES is the side-channel attack, which scans the system on which AES is implemented for information that can be exploited. [23] explains such an approach.

Conclusion

This chapter discussed block ciphers, more exactly the DES and AES algorithms. Despite the complexity of the mathematical background (which is not the main topic of the current work), we provided the main and foundational concepts on which block ciphers (e.g., DES and AES) are designed and built.

You learned about substitution and permutation networks, Feistel networks/cipher, round, substitution keys, round, initializing vectors, math concepts and terminology, etc. The most important goal of this chapter was to provide a way to explore a straightforward implementation of DES and AES in MATLAB.

This chapter is far from a comprehensive discussion of the theoretical aspects and practical side of cryptography, and for that reason, you are encouraged to follow the additional references indicated in this chapter.

References

[1]   Data Encryption System (DES) - FIPS Publication 46-3 `https://csrc.nist.gov/csrc/media/publications/fips/46/3/archive/1999-10-25/documents/fips46-3.pdf`.

[2]   Stinson, Douglas R., and Maura B. Paterson. *Cryptography: Theory and Practice*. Fourth edition, CRC Press, Taylor & Francis Group, 2019.

[3]   Atanasiu, Adrian. *Securitatea Informaţiei – Volumul 1: Criptografie.* InfoData, 2007. ISBN: 978-973-1803-16-6.

[4]   Menezes, A. J., et al. *Handbook of Applied Cryptography.* CRC Press, 1997.

[5]   Mihailescu, Marius Iulian, and Stefania Loredana Nita. *Pro Cryptography and Cryptanalysis: Creating Advanced Ciphers with C# and .NET.* Apress, 2021. *DOI.org (Crossref)*, doi:10.1007/978-1-4842-6367-9.

[6]   Mihailescu, Marius Iulian, and Stefania Loredana Nita. *Pro Cryptography and Cryptanalysis with C++20: Creating and Programming Advanced Ciphers.* Apress, 2021. DOI.org (Crossref), doi:10.1007/978-1-4842-6586-4.

[7]   Paar, Christof, and Jan Pelzl. *Understanding Cryptography: A Textbook for Students and Practitioners.* Springer Berlin Heidelberg, 2010. *DOI.org (Crossref)*, doi:10.1007/978-3-642-04101-3.

[8]   Schneier, Bruce. Applied Cryptography: Protocols, Ciphers, and Source Code in C. 20th anniversary edition, Wiley, 2015.

[9]   Stanoyevitch, Alexander. *Introduction to Cryptography with Mathematical Foundations and Computer Implementations.* CRC Press, 2011. ISBN: 979-8651423514.

[10] Z. Kukorelly, "The piling-up approximation in linear cryptanalysis," in *IEEE Transactions on Information Theory*, vol. 47, no. 7, pp. 2812-2823, Nov. 2001, doi: 10.1109/18.959262.

[11] Kukorelly Z. (1999) The Piling-Up Lemma and Dependent Random Variables. In: Walker M. (eds) Cryptography and Coding. Cryptography and Coding 1999. Lecture Notes in Computer Science, vol 1746. Springer, Berlin, Heidelberg. `https://doi.org/10.1007/3-540-46665-7_22`

[12] Harpes C., Kramer G.G., Massey J.L. (1995) *A Generalization of Linear Cryptanalysis and the Applicability of Matsui's Piling-up Lemma.* In: Guillou L.C., Quisquater JJ. (eds) Advances in

Cryptology — EUROCRYPT '95. EUROCRYPT 1995. Lecture Notes in Computer Science, vol 921. Springer, Berlin, Heidelberg. https://doi.org/10.1007/3-540-49264-X_3

[13]   Matsui M. (1994) Linear Cryptanalysis Method for DES Cipher. In: Helleseth T. (eds) Advances in Cryptology — EUROCRYPT '93. EUROCRYPT 1993. Lecture Notes in Computer Science, vol 765. Springer, Berlin, Heidelberg. https://doi.org/10.1007/3-540-48285-7_33

[14]   Pilling-up Lemma. Wikipedia - https://en.wikipedia.org/wiki/Piling-up_lemma.

[15]   Mister, S., et al. "Linear Approximation of Injective S-Boxes." *Electronics Letters*, vol. 31, no. 25, Dec. 1995, pp. 2165–66. *DOI.org (Crossref)*, doi:10.1049/el:19951466.

[16]   Chmiel K. (2006) On Differential and Linear Approximation of S-box Functions. In: Saeed K., Pejaś J., Mosdorf R. (eds) Biometrics, Computer Security Systems and Artificial Intelligence Applications. Springer, Boston, MA. https://doi.org/10.1007/978-0-387-36503-9_11

[17]   Howard M. Heys. A tutorial on linear and differential cryptanalysis, http://www.cs.bc.edu/~straubin/crypto2017/heys.pdf.

[18]   Announcing the ADVANCED ENCRYPTION STANDARD (AES). Federal Information Processing Standards Publication 197. United States National Institute of Standards and Technology (NIST). November 26, 2001. Archived (PDF) from the original on March 12, 2017. Retrieved October 2, 2012.

[19]   ISO/IEC 18033-3: Information technology – Security techniques – Encryption algorithms – Part 3: Block ciphers. Archived from the original on 2013-12-03.

[20]   Stallings, W. (2006). Cryptography and network security, 4/E. Pearson Education India.

[21]   AES-MATLAB, https://github.com/nick1au/AES-MATLAB

[22]   AES-Matlab, https://github.com/CaptainIRS/AES-Matlab

[23]   Ashokkumar, C., Giri, R. P., & Menezes, B. (2016, March). Highly efficient algorithms for AES key retrieval in cache access attacks. In 2016 IEEE European symposium on security and privacy (EuroS&P) (pp. 261-275). IEEE.

[24]   Data Encryption Standard (DES). Available online: https://www.mathworks.com/matlabcentral/fileexchange/37847-data-encryption-standard-des.

[25]   DES Encryption. Available online: https://www.mathworks.com/matlabcentral/fileexchange/53768-des-str-key-mode.

[26]   Data Encryption Standard (DES) in MATLAB. Available online: http://freesourcecode.net/matlabprojects/59871/data-encryption-standard-%28des%29-in-matlab

CHAPTER 10

Asymmetric Encryption Schemes

Asymmetric encryption is also called public key cryptography (PKC). In contrast to symmetric encryption, the cryptosystems in this category use a pair of keys, known as the *public key* and the *secret* (or *private*) *key*. Each key has a well-defined purpose. The public key encrypts the plain message and is available to anyone, whereas the secret key decrypts the ciphertext and is known only by the owner of the key.

Usually, in symmetric encryption, the algorithms are based on mathematical instruments such as permutations or substitutions, as you learned in the description of AES and DES. In asymmetric encryption, the mathematical tools are mostly asymmetric functions.

The first mention of public key cryptography is in a 1968 paper by Diffie and Hellman [1], in which they described how a public key cryptosystem should behave and how a public key distribution system should work to distribute secret keys between the involved parties over an insecure channel. At that time, this approach in cryptography had a great impact and was immediately followed by proposals in this direction.

Asymmetric encryption schemes need to meet some requirements:

- The pair of keys should be easily generated (from the computational point of view) by the secret key's owner (the receiver).

- The encryption process triggered by the sender should easily generate the encrypted text (from the computational point of view) from the plaintext (the message).

- The decryption process triggered by the receiver should easily recover the plaintext (from the computational point of view) from the encrypted text.

© Marius Iulian Mihailescu and Stefania Loredana Nita 2021
M. I. Mihailescu and S. L. Nita, *Cryptography and Cryptanalysis in MATLAB*,
https://doi.org/10.1007/978-1-4842-7334-0_10

- The secret key cannot be computed by knowing the public key.

- The plain message cannot be computed by knowing the public key and the encrypted text.

- One key is used only for encryption (the public one) and the other key is used only for decryption (the secret one).

A public key cryptosystem used by two parties, P_1 and P_2, works as follows:

1. Both P_1 and P_2 generate a pair of keys: the public key is available to everyone, while the secret key is kept private by each party.

2. When P_1 wants to send a message to P_2, it applies the encryption algorithm to the plain message using P_2's public key.

3. When P_2 receives the encrypted message from P_1, it applies the decryption algorithm to the encrypted message using its own secret key.

Some notable public key cryptosystems are RSA [2], ElGamal [3], and Merkle-Hellman [4], which we discuss in detail in the following sections. Asymmetric encryption has different applications, such as encryption schemes, hashes, digital certificates, digital signatures, encryption protocols, multi-party computation protocols, zero-knowledge proof protocols, and so on. Some important branches of asymmetric encryption are homomorphic encryption, searchable encryption, predicate encryption, and functional encryption, whereas branches of public key cryptography are integer factorization cryptography, elliptic-curve cryptography, lattice-based cryptography, learning and ring-learning with errors, multivariate cryptography, and code-based cryptography.

Asymmetric encryption schemes are often slower than symmetric ones with the same level of security. In such situations, it's preferred that the secret key of a symmetric encryption scheme be encrypted using an asymmetric cryptosystem and sent over an insecure channel, while the messages themselves are encrypted with the symmetric cryptosystem.

RSA

RSA is one of the first asymmetric encryption cryptosystems. It was proposed in [2] and it is widely adopted, even now. Its name came from the authors that proposed the encryption system, namely Ron Rivest, Adi Shamir, and Len Adleman.

The mathematical tool that is the basis for this cryptosystem, and therefore gives its security, is the integer factorization problem (or hardness assumption). In practice, it is difficult for a machine to factorize the product obtained by multiplying two large prime numbers. Usually, *difficult* means that the problem requires more than polynomial time to be solved. Let's look at the algorithms of the RSA cryptosystem as they were proposed in [2].

The *key generation algorithm* computes the private key and the secret key:

1. Randomly choose two large prime numbers, p, q.

2. Calculate the value $n = pq$.

3. Calculate the value $\phi(n)$, using the formula $\phi(n) = (p-1, q-1)$, where ϕ is Euler's totient function.

4. Pick an integer value e, with the properties $1 < e < \phi(n)$ and $\gcd(e, \phi(n)) = 1$, where *gcd* is the greatest common divisor between e and $\lambda(n)$.

5. Calculate $d \equiv e^{-1}(mod\ \phi(n))$.

With these values, the public key is $k_p = (n, e)$, and the secret key is $k_s = (p, q, \phi(n), d)$. Therefore, the encryption will involve the values n and e, while the decryption will involve the values $p, q, \phi(n)$ and d.

The *encryption algorithm* generates the encrypted message in just one step, by computing the encrypted value. Considering the integer value m, with the property $0 \le m < n$ being the plain message, its encryption c is obtained by using the following formula:

$$m^e \equiv c\,(mod\ n)$$

Similarly, the *decryption algorithm*, which recovers the plain message, has just one step. Considering the integer value c as the encrypted message, the corresponding plain message is obtained by using the following formula:

$$c^d \equiv \left(m^e\right)^d \equiv m\,(mod\ n)$$

Listing 10-1 is the MATLAB implementation of the RSA cryptosystem.

Listing 10-1. Implementation of the RSA Algorithm

```
1   clc;
2   disp('RSA Algorithm');
3   clear all; close all;
4
5   %p = input('\nEnter the first prime number (p) : ');
6   %q = input('Enter the second prime number (q) : ');
7
8   p=generate_prime(sym(2)^10,sym(2)^11);
9   fprintf('Computed value (p): %d\n', p);
10
11   q=generate_prime(sym(2)^10,sym(2)^11);
12   fprintf('Computed value (q): %d \n', q);
13
14   fprintf('\n')
15
16   n=p*q;
17   fprintf('Computed value (n): %d\n', n);
18
19   phi_n=(p-1)*(q-1);
20   fprintf('Computed value (phi_n): %d\n', phi_n);
21
22   e=-1;
23   val=round(1+(phi_n-1)*rand(1,1));
24   if gcd(val,phi_n) ~= 1
25       while gcd(val,phi_n) ~= 1 || val ==1
26           val=round(1+(phi_n-1)*rand(1,1));
27           if gcd(val,phi_n) == 1
28               e=val;
29               break;
30           end
31       end
32   end
33
```

```
34    fprintf('Computed value (e): %d\n', e);

35

36    [aux, aux2, ~] = gcd(e,phi_n);
37    if aux==1
38        d = mod(aux2,phi_n);
39        fprintf('Computed value (d): %d\n', d);
40    else
41        disp('Value (d) cannot be computed');
42    end

43

44    fprintf('\n');
45    fprintf('Public key: (%d, %d)\n', n, e);
46    fprintf('Public key: (%d, %d, %d, %d)\n', p, q, phi_n, d);

47

48

49    plain_message = input('\nEnter the message to be sent (m < n):');

50

51    if plain_message>n
52        disp('The message (m) should be less than (n).');
53        return;
54    end
55    encrypted_message=power(sym(plain_message), e);
56    encrypted_message=mod(encrypted_message, n);
57    disp('Encrypted message:   ');
58    disp(encrypted_message);

59

60    decrypted_message=power(sym(encrypted_message), d);
61    decrypted_message=mod(decrypted_message, n);
62    disp('Decrypted message:   ');
63    disp(decrypted_message);

64

65    function q = generate_prime(a,b)
66        aux=round(a+(b-a)*rand(1,1));
67        while is_prime(aux) == 0
68            aux=round(a+(b-a)*rand(1,1));
```

```
69          end
70          q=aux;
71    end
72
73    function check=is_prime(x)
74        check=1;
75        for i = 2:sqrt(x)
76            if mod(x,i) == 0
77                check=0;
78                return;
79            end
80        end
81    end
```

The implementation follows the steps of the RSA algorithm. Lines 5-46 implement the key generation algorithm. The values p, q are random numbers generated using the generate_prime function (Lines 65-71), which randomly generates a number and determines whether it is a prime (Lines 73-81). Another option is that the user can insert values for p and q according to Step 1 of the key generation algorithm (the commented code on Lines 5 and 6). Lines 22-32 compute the value of variable e from Step 4 of the key generation algorithm. In lines 36-42, we compute the value d. There, the inverse of e is computed based on the fact that it exists only if $gcd\,(e, \phi(n)) = 1$. Next, the user inserts the message that will be encrypted. The message is an integer value less than n. Lines 55-58 compute the encrypted value and display it. The encryption is quite simple; the power and mod functions are applied according to the encryption function. Finally, Lines 60-63 decrypt the encrypted message obtained previously and display it, by applying the power and mod functions according to the decryption function. Figure 10-1 shows the result of the implementation.

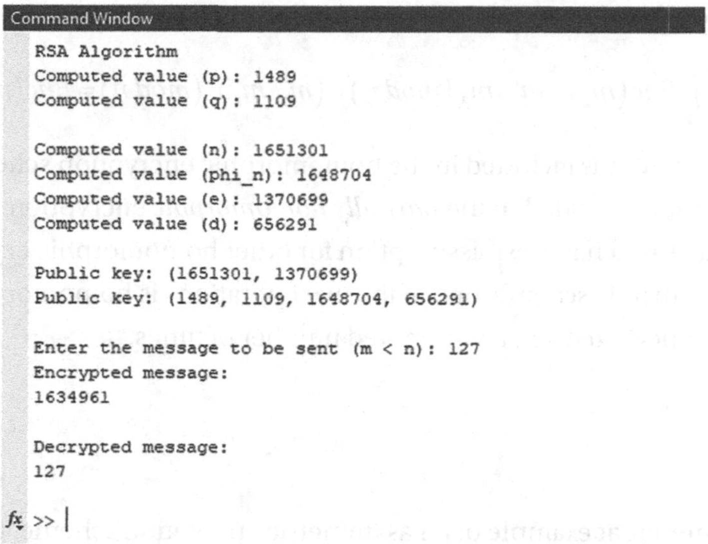

```
Command Window

   RSA Algorithm
   Computed value (p): 1489
   Computed value (q): 1109

   Computed value (n): 1651301
   Computed value (phi_n): 1648704
   Computed value (e): 1370699
   Computed value (d): 656291

   Public key: (1651301, 1370699)
   Public key: (1489, 1109, 1648704, 656291)

   Enter the message to be sent (m < n): 127
   Encrypted message:
   1634961

   Decrypted message:
   127

fx >> |
```

Figure 10-1. *The result of the RSA implementation*

Note that we wrote our own function to generate and check the primality of a number. But in real-life applications—primality tests, such as Miller-Rabin or Fermat [9], and randomness tests, such as Diehard [10] or NIST battery tests [11]—are crucial in cryptography.

The RSA cryptosystem is one of the most important asymmetric encryptions in cryptography. As you have seen, its security lies in its factorization problem. From RSA was born the RSA problem, which has become a hardness assumption for many other encryption systems. The RSA problem represents the labor of computing the RSA private key knowing the public key. At the moment of writing this book, there is no efficient algorithm that performs this task for an RSA cryptosystem with a key larger than 1024 bits.

The RSA cryptosystem is interesting from another point of view: it has homomorphic properties. *Homomorphic encryption* is of interest in cryptography at this moment, because it allows computations to be applied directly over encrypted data. Many years ago, these properties were considered weaknesses of an encryption scheme because an attacker could alter the encrypted text, but things changed because this actually has many benefits and has proved to be secure following some rules. For more information about homomorphic encryption, consult reference [5].

The homomorphic operation of RSA is the following multiplication:

$$Enc(m_1) \cdot Enc(m_2) = m_1^e \cdot m_2^e \ (mod \ n) = (m_1 \cdot m_2)^e \ (mod \ n) = Enc(m_1 \cdot m_2)$$

Due to this fact, RSA is included in the homomorphic encryption schemes category. More specifically, it is included in the *partially homomorphic* encryption schemes, and it represents a basis or a hardness assumption for other homomorphic cryptosystems. In a partially homomorphic scheme, one of the two operations is homomorphic, and it can be applied to the encrypted text an unlimited number of times.

ElGamal

ElGamal is another great example of an asymmetric encryption scheme, and it was proposed in 1985 by Taher ElGamal. The mathematical tools used in ElGamal cryptosystems are cyclic groups and security is based on two hardness assumptions related to the discrete logarithm problem (more technical details are found in reference [6]) called computational Diffie-Hellman assumption and decisional Diffie-Hellman assumption (more technical details are found in references [7]). We next present the algorithms of the ElGamal cryptosystem as proposed in reference [3].

The *key generation algorithm* computes the private key and the secret key. It has the following steps:

1.   Choose a cyclic group G, generated by the element $g \in G$ and with the order q, where q is a prime number. The neutral element of G is e.

2.   Pick an integer value $x \in \{1, ..., q-1\}$.

3.   Calculate the value $h = gx$.

With these values, the public key is $k_p = (G, q, g, h)$ and the secret key is $k_s = x$.

The encryption algorithm generates the encrypted message and has more steps. Treating the plain message as a value $m \in G$, the sender proceeds as follows:

1.   Randomly choose an integer value $y \in \{1, ...q-1\}$.

2.   Calculate the value $s = hy$.

3.   Calculate the value $c_1 = gy$.

4.   Calculate the value $c_2 = m \cdot s$.

The encrypted message is represented by the pair $c = (c_1, c_2)$.

The decryption algorithm recovers the initial message and has more steps. Considering the encrypted message being the pair $c = (c_1, c_2)$, the receiver proceeds as follows:

1. Calculate the value $s = c_1^x$.

2. Calculate the inverse element of s, namely s^{-1}.

3. Calculate $m = c_2 \cdot s^{-1}$.

The initial message is always recovered because indeed, $c_2 \cdot s^{-1} = (m \cdot s) \cdot s^{-1} = m$.

Note that all operations from the algorithms are made within group G, so all values used remain in G.

Observe that in Step 3 of encryption, the value s is computed, which is known as the *shared secret*. It is called this, because upon look and with some easy verifications, the same value is obtained in Step 1 on decryption: $c_1^x = \left(g^y\right)^x = g^{xy} = h^y$. Therefore, the sender and the receiver work with the same secret value, hy.

If an attacker knows $c = (c_1, c_2)$ and manages to obtain the corresponding plain message m, the shared secret can easily be calculated: $c_2 \cdot m^{-1} = s$. For this reason, every time a plain message m is encrypted, a new value y needs to be chosen.

To compute the inverse in a cyclic group, different algorithms can be used. For example, the extended Euclidean algorithm is a good, easy approach. Listing 10-2 presents the MATLAB implementation of the ElGamal cryptosystem.

Listing 10-2. ElGamal Implementation

```
1    clc;
2    disp('ElGamal Algorithm');
3    clear all; close all;
4    q=generate_prime(sym(2)^10,sym(2)^11);
5    disp('Computed value (q):  ');
6    disp(q)
7
8    g=round(1+((q-1)-1)*rand(1,1));
9    disp('Computed value (g):  ');
10   disp(g);
11
12   x=round(1+((q-1)-1)*rand(1,1));
```

```
13    disp('Computed value (x):   ');
14    disp(x);
15
16    h=power(sym(g),x);
17    disp('Computed value (h):   ');
18    disp(h);
19
20    plain_message = input('\nEnter the message to be sent (m <q): ');
21
22    if plain_message>q
23        disp('The message (m) should be less than (q).');
24        return;
25    end
26
27    fprintf('\nEncrypting...\n');
28
29    y=round(1+((q-1)-1)*rand(1,1));
30    disp('Computed value (y):   ');
31    disp(y);
32
33    s=power(sym(h),y);
34    disp('Computed value (s) [shared secret - sender]:   ');
35    disp(s);
36
37    c1=power(sym(g),y);
38    disp('Computed value (c1):   ');
39    disp(c1);
40
41    c2=plain_message*s;
42    disp('Computed value (c2):   ');
43    disp(c2);
44
45    disp('Encrypted message has two components:   ');
46    fprintf('      c1 = %sym.\n', c1);
47    fprintf('      c2 = %sym.\n', c2);
```

```
48
49    fprintf('\nDecrypting...');
50
51    ss=power(sym(c1),x);
52    fprintf('\nComputed value (ss) [shared secret - receiver]:    53    ');
54    disp(ss);
55
56    inv_s = compute_inverse(ss,q);
57    if inv_s == -1
58        disp('Wrong setup. Retry.');
59        return;
60    end
61    disp('Computed value (ss^-1):  ');
62    disp(inv_s);
63
64    decrypted_message=mod(c2*inv_s,q);
65    disp('Decrypted message  ');
66    disp(decrypted_message);
67
68    function q = generate_prime(a,b)
69        aux=round(a+(b-a)*rand(1,1));
70        while is_prime(aux) == 0
71            aux=round(a+(b-a)*rand(1,1));
72        end
73        q=aux;
74    end
75
76    function check=is_prime(x)
77        check=1;
78        for i = 2:sqrt(x)
79            if mod(x,i) == 0
80                check=0;
81                return;
82            end
83        end
84    end
```

```
85
86    function inv = compute_inverse(a,b)
87        [aux, aux2, ~] = gcd(a,b);
88        if aux==1
89            inv = mod(aux2,b);
90        else
91            inv = -1;
92        end
93    end
```

The implementation is quite simple and self-explanatory, as the steps of the algorithm are strictly followed. In Lines 4-18, the keys are generated and the values q, g, x, h are computed and displayed. To generate the prime number q, we used the generate_prime function (Lines 68-74), which randomly generates an integer in a range and determines whether it is prime using the is_prime function (Lines 76-84). Then, the user must introduce the message that needs to be encrypted in the form of a number less than q. In Lines 29-47, the values needed for encryption are computed and displayed, obtaining the encrypted message in the form of the pair (c_1, c_2). The last step is decryption, which is in Lines 51-66, where the necessary values are computed and displayed. Finally, the decrypted message is displayed. Figure 10-2 shows the result of the implementation.

```
Command Window

ElGamal Algorithm
Computed value (q):
1373

Computed value (g):
803

Computed value (x):
308

Computed value (h):
44914642353996972934553230832774913793758119563894640630823421652071919556360502458620070439887599716849691227021447175368621993997928829765122400327236159609071398

Enter the message to be sent (m < q): 35

Encrypting...
Computed value (y):
1031

Computed value (s) [shared secret - sender]:
40923442022695605436619463054225366538853123422532819853590474881255971954677173202693707149120221002771678389647015797522346259026549004538867905790931410273477010

Computed value (c1):
57773300964616491212137865217256313473995651456449910632044603728892082978006335659663063117670796501022343054457786900674267374987036052724847276548281908224558752

Computed value (c2):
14323204707943461902816812068978878288598593197886486948756666208439590184137010620942797502192077350970087436376455529132821190659292151588603767026825993595716953

Encrypted message has two components:
    c1 = 57773300964616491212137865217256313473995651456449910632044603728892082978006335659663063117670796501022343054457786900674267374987036052724847276548281908
    c2 = 14323204707943461902816812068978878288598593197886486948756666208439590184137010620942797502192077350970087436376455529132821190659292151588603767026825998

Decrypting...
Computed value (ss) [shared secret - receiver]:   40923442022695605436619463054225366538853123422532819853590474881255971954677173202693707149120221002771678389647010

Computed value (ss^-1):
365

Decrypted message
35

fx >> |
```

Figure 10-2. *The result of the ElGamal implementation*

Note that in this implementation we used sym to work with large numbers. As with the RSA algorithm, note that we wrote our own function that generates and checks the primality of a number. In real-life applications, primality tests—such as Miller-Rabin or Fermat [9], and randomness tests, such as Diehard [10] or NIST battery tests [11]—are crucial in cryptography.

As you have seen, ElGamal is another great example of an asymmetric encryption scheme. Similar to RSA, ElGamal has homomorphic properties and is included in the partially homomorphic encryption scheme category. The homomorphic property is as follows:

$$Enc(m_1) \cdot Enc(m_2) = \left(g^{y_1}, m_1 \cdot h^{y_1}\right) \cdot \left(g^{y_2}, m_2 \cdot h^{y_2}\right) = \left(g^{y_1} \cdot g^{y_2}, m_1 \cdot h^{y_1} \cdot m_2 \cdot h^{y_2}\right) =$$
$$\left(g^{y_1 y_2}, \left(m_1 m_2\right) \cdot h^{y_1 y_2}\right) = Enc(m_1 \cdot m_2)$$

Merkle-Hellman

The last example of an asymmetric encryption presented in this chapter is the Merkle-Hellman cryptosystem [4]. It is proved in reference [8] that this cryptosystem is insecure, but it is notable because of the ingenious approach it uses, called the knapsack approach, which is discussed in the next section.

Knapsack Approach

The Knapsack problem is a classical problem in combinatorial optimization, and it has the following statement: given a knapsack with a maximum supported weight and a set of objects for which the value of each object and the weight of each object are known, the requirement is to fill the knapsack without exceeding the maximum weight and to obtain the highest profit possible.

The knapsack problem has two variations: the *discrete* problem, whereby only whole objects may be used, and the *continuous* problem, whereby whole objects and fractions of objects may be used.

From a technical point of view, the knapsack problem can be formulated as follows, Given a set of integers $A = \{a_1, ... a_n\}$ and a value S, find the values $X = \{x_1, ..., x_n\}$, $x_i \in [0, 1]$, such that $S = a_1x_1 + ... + a_nx_n$. Because in cryptography the units are bits, the possible values for x_i are 0 and 1.

The Algorithms

In this section, we present the algorithms of the Merkle-Hellman cryptosystem.

The key generation algorithm computes the private key and the secret key. It has the following steps:

1. Choose an integer value n that will represent the dimension of the block.

2. Randomly choose a set of n values of positive integers $W = \{w_1, ..., w_n\}$ with the following property $w_k > \sum_{i=1}^{k-1} w_i, 1 < k \leq n$.

3. Randomly choose the integer value q with the following property:
   $$q > \sum_{i=1}^{n} w_i.$$

4. Randomly choose the integer value r with the following property: $\gcd(r, q) = 1$.

5. Compute the element of the tuple $B = (b_1, ..., b_n)$, $b_i = rw_i \bmod q$.

With these values, the public key is $k_p = B$ and the secret key is $k_s = (W, q, r)$.

The encryption algorithm generates the encrypted message. Considering the plain message is a value $m = m_1...m_n$, where m_i is a bit and m_1 is the most significant bit, the sender should compute the following value:

$$c = \sum_{i=1}^{n} m_i b_i$$

The encrypted message is represented by the value c.

The decryption algorithm recovers the initial message and has more steps. Considering the encrypted message is the value c, the receiver proceeds as follows:

1. Compute the inverse element of r, namely $r' = r^{-1}(\bmod q)$.

2. Compute the value $c' = cr'(\bmod q)$.

3. Find the subset $X = \{x_1, ...x_k\}$ such that $c' = \sum_{i=1}^{k} w_i x_i$.

4. Recover the initial message by computing $m = \sum_{i=1}^{k} 2^{n-x_i}$.

Note that the problem in Step 3 is called the subset sum problem for the value c', and it can be solved using a greedy algorithm.

Conclusion

This chapter discussed asymmetric encryption. It's also called public key cryptography, because it uses a pair of keys, a public key for encryption and a secret (or private) key for decryption. However, the asymmetric cryptosystems should meet some requirements that we listed at the beginning of the chapter and there are some steps that need to be followed.

The chapter also discussed three of the most important classical asymmetric cryptosystems—RSA, ElGamal, and Merkle-Hellman, and it implemented the algorithms for RSA and ElGamal. An important general comment is that the prime numbers should be generated using powerful pseudo-random number generators, and their primality should be tested using powerful primality tests, because randomness and primality are important concepts in cryptography.

References

[1]   Diffie, W., & Hellman, M. (1976). *New directions in cryptography.* IEEE transactions on Information Theory, 22(6), 644-654.

[2]   Rivest, R. L., Shamir, A., & Adleman, L. (1978). *A method for obtaining digital signatures and public-key cryptosystems.* Communications of the ACM, 21(2), 120-126.

[3]   ElGamal, T. (1985). *A public key cryptosystem and a signature scheme based on discrete logarithms.* IEEE transactions on information theory, 31(4), 469-472.

[4]   Merkle, R., & Hellman, M. (1978). *Hiding information and signatures in trapdoor knapsacks.* IEEE transactions on Information Theory, 24(5), 525-530.

[5]   Acar, A., Aksu, H., Uluagac, A. S., & Conti, M. (2018). *A survey on homomorphic encryption schemes: Theory and implementation.* *ACM Computing Surveys* (CSUR), 51(4), 1-35.

[6]   McCurley, K. S. (1990). *The discrete logarithm problem. In Proc. of Symp. in Applied Math* (Vol. 42, pp. 49-74).

[7]   Bao, F., Deng, R. H., & Zhu, H. (2003, October). *Variations of diffie-hellman problem. In International conference on information and communications security* (pp. 301-312). Springer, Berlin, Heidelberg.

[8]   Shamir, A. (1982, November). *A polynomial time algorithm for breaking the basic Merkle-Hellman cryptosystem.* In 23rd Annual Symposium on Foundations of Computer Science (sfcs 1982) (pp. 145-152). IEEE.

[9]   Primality test. Available online: https://en.wikipedia.org/wiki/Primality_test

[10] Diehard tests. Available online: https://en.wikipedia.org/wiki/Diehard_tests

[11]   Rukhin, A., Soto, J., Nechvatal, J., Barker, E., Leigh, S., Levenson, M., ... & Iii, L. E. B. (2002). *A statistical test suite for random and pseudorandom number generators for cryptographic applications*, NIST Special Publication 800-22. Available online: `https://nvlpubs.nist.gov/nistpubs/Legacy/SP/nistspecialpublication800-22r1a.pdf`

CHAPTER 11

Formal Techniques for Cryptography

Cryptography uses mathematical concepts to design strong cryptosystems and make cryptanalyses for them. Cryptography uses number theory, probability theory, and information theory. We talked about number theory in Chapter 5, therefore, in this chapter, we present the main ideas of the probability theory used in cryptography.

Probability Theory

This section introduces the basic concepts of probability theory that are used in cryptography, such as experiments, events, and distributions. The definitions and formulas within this section are compiled from resources [1]-[3]. Any of these resources can be considered further readings or as good resources for more comprehensive technical aspects. Let's first define some terms:

- *Experiment.* A process that discovers something or tests an assumption is called an experiment. In probabilities, an experiment has an output from a set of outputs that are individual. The set of outputs is called the sample space (often denoted as G), and the outputs that can result from an experiment are called simple events (often denoted $g_1, g_2, ..., g_n$).

- *Probability distribution.* A set of positive numbers $S = \{s_1, ..., s_n\}$, $\sum_{i=1}^{n} s_i = 1$ is called a probability distribution over G and s_i represents the probability of the event g_i to occur under a given experiment.

© Marius Iulian Mihailescu and Stefania Loredana Nita 2021
M. I. Mihailescu and S. L. Nita, *Cryptography and Cryptanalysis in MATLAB*,
https://doi.org/10.1007/978-1-4842-7334-0_11

- *Event*. A subset of the sample space G is called an event and is often denoted E and the probability for E to occur is denoted as $P(E)$. In this case, $P(E) = \sum_{i=1}^{k} s_i$, where $E = \{s_1, ..., s_k\} \subseteq O$. A complementary event is the set of all simple events that are not contained by E, namely $\bar{E} = S - E$, therefore $\bar{E} \cup E = S$ and $\bar{E} \cap E = \varnothing$.

The following properties occur:

1. $0 \le P(E) \le 1, (\forall) E$

2. $P(S) = 1$ and $P(\varnothing) = 0$

3. $P(\bar{E}) = 1 - P(E)$

4. If the simple events of S have the same probability of apparition, then $P(E) = \dfrac{|E|}{|S|}$.

- *Mutually exclusive events*. Two events E_1, E_2 are called mutually exclusive if $P(E_1 \cap E_2) = 0$. If event E_1 takes place, then for sure E_2 will not take place and vice versa.

The following properties occur for two events E_1 and E_2:

1. $P(E_1) \le P(E_2)$ when $E_1 \subseteq P(E_2)$.

2. $P(E_1 \cup E_2) + P(E_1 \cap E_2) = P(E_1) + P(E_2)$

3. $P(E_1 \cup E_2) = P(E_1) + P(E_2)$ when E_1 and E_2 are mutually exclusive.

- *Conditional probability*. Let E_1, E_2 be two events, with $P(E_2) > 0$. The occurrence of event E_2 is conditioned by the occurrence of event E_1, which is called conditional probability and is written as $P(E_1|E_2)$. It has the following formula:

$$P(E_1|E_2) = \frac{P(E_1 \cap E_2)}{P(E_2)}$$

The events are considered to be independent if $P(E_1 \cap E_2) = P(E_1)P(E_2)$.

- *Bayes' Theorem*. Considering two events E_1, E_2, with $P(E_2) > 0$, the following relationship takes place:

$$P(E_1|E_2) = \frac{P(E_1)P(E_2|E_1)}{P(E_2)}.$$

Random Variables

Random variables are mathematical concepts that study the random phenomenon. To do so, some elements should be defined from a technical point of view. Therefore in this section, we present the definitions that imply random variables.

- *Random variable.* A random variable is a function $X: S \to \mathbb{R}$ that maps the elements of the probability distribution to elements of the real number set.

- *Mean.* Considering X a random variable, the mean of X (or the expected value of X) is given by the formula:

$$E(X) = \sum_{s_i \in S} X(s_i) P(s_i)$$

- *Variance.* Considering X a random variable, its mean $\mu = E(X)$, then the variance of X is given by the formula:

$$Var(X) = E\left((X - \mu)^2\right)$$

    Often, the variance is denoted with σ^2.

- *Standard deviation.* Considering X a random variable, its variance $Var(X)$, then the standard deviation of X is given by the formula:

$$\sigma = \sqrt{\sigma^2}$$

Birthday Problem

In this section, we present the birthday problem, which is base for the brute-force birthday attack in cryptography. Before describing the problem, let's define some concepts.

Considering two natural numbers a, b with $a \geq b$, the number $a^{(b)}$ is defined as

$$a^{(b)} = a(a-1)(a-2)\ldots(a-b+1)$$

Second-type Stirling number. Considering two natural numbers $a, b, a \geq b$, the Second-type Stirling number is denoted $\begin{Bmatrix} a \\ b \end{Bmatrix}$ and has the following formula:

$$\begin{Bmatrix} a \\ b \end{Bmatrix} = \frac{1}{b!} \sum_{i=0}^{n} (-1)^{b-i} \binom{b}{i} i^a$$

An exception is the Stirling number $\begin{Bmatrix} 0 \\ 0 \end{Bmatrix}$ for which the value is $\begin{Bmatrix} 0 \\ 0 \end{Bmatrix} = 1$, and the Stirling number $\begin{Bmatrix} a \\ a \end{Bmatrix} = 1$

Occupancy problem. Consider an urn that contains a balls, which are labeled with numbers from 1 to a. From here, b balls are extracted one at a time and replaced at the same time, and with their numbers listed. The probability to pick l different balls is given by the following formula:

$$P_1(a, b, l) = \begin{Bmatrix} b \\ l \end{Bmatrix} \frac{a^{(l)}}{a^b}, 1 \leq l \leq b$$

Next, consider an urn that contains a balls, which are labeled with numbers from 1 to a, from where b balls are extracted one at a time and replaced at the same time, and with their numbers listed. The following cases can take place:

(1) The probability for at least one coincidence is given by the formula:

$$P_2(a, b) = 1 - P_1(a, b, b) = 1 - \begin{Bmatrix} b \\ b \end{Bmatrix} \frac{a^{(b)}}{a^b} = 1 - \frac{a^{(b)}}{a^b}, 1 \leq b \leq a$$

(2) If $b = O(\sqrt{a})$ and $a \to \infty$, then the probability for at least one coincidence is given by the formula:

$$P_2(a, b) \to 1 - \exp\left(-\frac{b(b-1)}{2a} + O\left(\frac{1}{\sqrt{a}} \right) \right) \approx 1 - \exp\left(-\frac{b^2}{2a} \right)$$

For case (2), the notation $O(\cdot)$ represents an *asymptotic bound*. In brief, $f(x) = O(g(x))$ reflects the fact that f grows faster than g with at most asymptotic growth.

The birthday problem is a particular case of the occupancy problem, which states that in a random set of 23 individuals, the probability that two individuals have the same birthdate is at least ½. With these concepts, this probability is

$$P_2(365, 23) \approx 0.507$$

In this formula, a=365, because there are 365 possible values for a birthdate, and b=23, because 23 is the number of individuals.

Entropy

In this section, we discuss the entropy of random variables. For this section, consider the random variables Y, Z and a random variable X defined by the finite set $\{x_1, ..., x_n\}$. If the probability that X takes the value x_1 is denoted $P(X = x_i) = p_i$, $0 \leq p_i \leq 1$, then

$$\sum_{i=1}^{n} p_i = 1$$

Informally, the entropy of a random variable X is a mathematical concept that measures the "quantity" of the information provided within an observation x. The entropy can be computed using this formula:

$$H(X) = -\sum_{i=1}^{n} p_i \lg p_i = \sum_{i=1}^{n} p_i \lg\left(\frac{1}{p_i}\right)$$

If $p_i = 0$, by convention $p_i \lg p_i = p_i \lg\left(\frac{1}{p_i}\right) = 0$.

Joint entropy. Considering X, Y two random variables, their joint entropy is given by the formula:

$$H(X, Y) = \sum_{x, y} P(X = x, Y = y) \lg\left(P(X = x, Y = y)\right),$$

where x and y iterate all values for the random variables X, Y.

(Conditional entropy). Considering X, Y two random variables, the conditional entropy of X when $Y = y$ is given by the formula:

$$H(X|Y = y) = -\sum_{x} P(X = x|Y = y) \lg\left(P(X = x|Y = y)\right)$$

where x iterates all values for the random variable X. The conditional entropy is also called equivocation *of Y about X,* and from this point of view it is expressed as follows:

$$H(X|Y) = \sum_y P(Y = y) H(X|Y = y),$$

where y iterates all values for the random variables Y.

MATLAB implements a wide range of functions within the probability theory. A comprehensive list of such functions can be found in [4].

Randomness in Cryptography

Another extremely important concept in cryptography is *randomness*, because it is related to unpredictability. Randomness can be achieved through hardware components that are non-deterministic, called true random number generators (TRNG). Randomness can also be achieved algorithmically, using pseudorandom number generators (PRNG), which are deterministic.

There are several standards that describe how these should be constructed and implemented and provide tests for randomness. Some of them are RFC 4086 [5], FIPS Pub 140-2 [6], and NIST Special Publication 800-90b [7]. All major professional associations—such as IETF, IEEE, NIST, ANSI, and ISO—have proposed standards for randomness.

From a mathematical point of view, a pseudorandom number generator is actually a function of the following form [8]:

$$f : K \times \mathbb{N} \to \mathbb{Z}_2,$$

where K is an algebraic structure with the following properties:

(1) f is an easily computable function.

(2) It is difficult to determine k knowing $\underbrace{f(k,1),\dots,f(k,n)}_{(*)}$.

(3) It is difficult to determine $f(k, n + 1)$, $f(k, n + 2)$, ... knowing $\underbrace{f(k,1),\dots,f(k,n)}_{(*)}$.

PRNGs use an initial value called a "seed" that instantiates them. The problem with PRNGs is that when their internal state is known, the values that they output become predictable. However, PRNGs are efficient when they are implemented properly and work in certain conditions (for example, those defined in the standards). They are important because:

- An attacker cannot predict the outputs of a PRNG as long as the internal state of the PRNG remains unknown.

- The information that is leaked by the outputs of a PRNG is minimum and limited. From this fact, the PRNG should change the seed periodically. Note that the seed itself should be randomly chosen.

- PRNGs are easier to implement than TRNGs and a well-seeded PRNG generates output quickly.

Sometimes the data that feed PRNGs introduces bias in the output, because the chances for bits to be outputted are inequal. Namely, "1" is more likely to be output than "0" and vice versa. This is a vulnerable point, and this situation should be eliminated with post-processing, so that both bits have the same chances of being outputted.

Further, we present an example of how to generate pseudorandom numbers. In this example, we generate some independent runs for a generic experiment.

In Line 4 of Listing 11-1, we used the rng function to specify the seed for the generator. This function controls the seed for the generators such as rand or randn. In Line 6, we specified how many runs we need and, in Line 7, we specified how many experiments per run we need. Therefore, we will have in total times×noOfExp random values, which are stored in the randNums variable. The result is shown in Figure 11-1.

```
Command Window                                                          —  □  ×
Generating numbers...
    0.8701    0.5562    0.3261    0.5142    0.6696    0.0771    0.0887    0.6551    0.8422    0.5909
    0.5823    0.3671    0.6992    0.5591    0.4561    0.6449    0.6417    0.6021    0.4408    0.1637
    0.2788    0.4024    0.3664    0.0344    0.2898    0.3093    0.1324    0.7191    0.3740    0.8369
    0.1859    0.1130    0.8364    0.7199    0.5258    0.5243    0.7665    0.4152    0.9137    0.7752
    0.4111    0.4470    0.4813    0.4210    0.5592    0.9581    0.0767    0.3965    0.5478    0.1690
    0.1174    0.5854    0.5165    0.4369    0.7453    0.8832    0.3310    0.8251    0.2519    0.7670
    0.6850    0.1620    0.3830    0.2817    0.8283    0.2954    0.6799    0.7126    0.0275    0.3354
    0.4376    0.5207    0.9975    0.9003    0.8237    0.5124    0.5092    0.0979    0.2063    0.4724
fx >> |
```

Figure 11-1. *The result of Listing 11-1*

Listing 11-1. Generating Independent Runs for an Experiment

```
1   clc;
2   disp('Generating numbers...');
3   clear all; close all;
4
5   rng(25);
6   times = 8;
7   noOfExp = 10;
8   randNums = rand(times,noOfExp);
9   disp(randNums);
```

Note that rand generates values in the interval [0,1] and they are uniformly distributed. To generate *integer* numbers in a specific interval, we proceed as shown in Listing 11-2.

Listing 11-2. Generating Independent Runs in a Specific Interval

```
1    clc;
2    disp('Generating numbers interval...');
3    clear all; close all;
4
5    rng(25);
6    times = 8;
7    noOfExp = 10;
8    minVal = 100;
9    maxVal = 1000;
10   randNums = round(minVal+(maxVal-minVal)*rand(times,noOfExp));
11   disp(randNums);
```

The difference from the initial code is represented in Lines 8, 9, and 10, where we specified the limits of the interval and used a formula to generate that interval. The result is shown in Figure 11-2.

```
Command Window                                                    —   □   ×

Generating numbers interval...
   883   601   393   563   703   169   180   690   858   632
   624   430   729   603   510   680   678   642   497   247
   351   462   430   131   361   378   219   747   437   853
   267   202   853   748   573   572   790   474   922   798
   470   502   533   479   603   962   169   457   593   252
   206   627   565   493   771   895   398   843   327   790
   716   246   445   354   846   366   712   741   125   402
   494   569   998   910   841   561   558   188   286   525

fx >> |
```

Figure 11-2. *The result of Listing 11-2*

Conclusion

This chapter presented the main ideas around the probability theory used in cryptography, including probability properties, random variables, and entropy. The birthday problem was presented because it is the mathematical base for the brute-force birthday attack. Finally, the random number generators were presented and you saw how random numbers can be generated in MATLAB.

References

[1]   Menezes, A. J., Van Oorschot, P. C., & Vanstone, S. A. (2018). *Handbook of applied cryptography.* CRC press.

[2]   Johnson, R. A., Miller, I., & Freund, J. E. (2000). *Probability and statistics for engineers* (Vol. 2000, p. 642p). London: Pearson Education.

[3]   Rohatgi, V. K., & Saleh, A. M. E. (2015). *An introduction to probability and statistics.* John Wiley & Sons.

[4]   Probability Distributions — Functions, https://www.mathworks.com/help/stats/referencelist.html?type=function&listtype=cat&category=probability-distributions-1&blocktype=all&capability=&s_tid=CRUX_lftnav

[5] Randomness Requirements for Security, 2005. Available online: https://datatracker.ietf.org/doc/html/rfc4086

[6] Security Requirements for Cryptographic Modules, Available online: https://csrc.nist.gov/publications/detail/fips/140/2/final

[7] Recommendation for the Entropy Sources Used for Random Bit Generation, Available online: https://csrc.nist.gov/publications/detail/sp/800-90b/final

[8] Ferguson, N., & Schneier, B. (2003). *Practical cryptography* (Vol. 141). New York: Wiley.

CHAPTER 12

Visual Cryptography

So far you have seen several different approaches to cryptography. In this chapter, we discuss the "visual side" of cryptography, in which a message is encrypted under an image and deciphering is done by the human eye.

Visual cryptography is a cryptographic technique in which the encrypted message can be decrypted only by being seen "with the sight." With visual cryptography, various inputs can be encrypted, namely text, images, documents, etc.

This encryption technique was introduced by Naor and Shamir in [1]. In their paper, the authors proposed a secret sharing scheme that works as follows: the encrypted image is partitioned in n parts that are sent individually and the encrypted image can be decrypted only when all of the n parts (or *shares*) are put together. In addition, if someone has $n - 1$ parts, nothing can be learned from these about the original image. For each part, a different degree of transparency is set and the decryption consists of overlaying the n parts. This is where sight is involved: namely, the decrypted image is seen by the human eye after the parts are overlapped. When this is accomplished, the original image is recovered. Since its introduction, different schemes from visual cryptography have been proposed, including black and white and colored images [2] [3]. Visual cryptography has different applications, including secret communication, copyrights, authentication of documents, etc.

An initial approach is two out of n sharing technique, which means there is an arbitrary number (n) of entities that share a secret, but at least two entities are allowed to decrypt the secret. In the scheme proposed in [1], the n parts represent the secret image with random degrees of transparency and revealing nothing about the original secret image. If any two parts are overlaid, the original secret image can be deciphered by the human eye. The secret image should have a binary image, which is represented as pixels. From the secret image, a pixel is represented as subpixels organized in the form of

M. I. Mihailescu and S. L. Nita, *Cryptography and Cryptanalysis in MATLAB*, https://doi.org/10.1007/978-1-4842-7334-0_12

matrices that determine the color of the main pixel. For example, in [1], a white pixel of the secret image is encoded in each part (or share) using a permutation of the following matrix:

$$C_0 = \begin{bmatrix} 1 & 0 & \dots & 0 \\ 1 & 0 & \dots & 0 \\ \dots & \dots & \dots & \dots \\ 1 & 0 & \dots & 0 \end{bmatrix}$$

The black pixel is represented by permutations of the following matrix:

$$C_1 = \begin{bmatrix} 1 & 0 & \dots & 0 \\ 0 & 1 & \dots & 0 \\ \dots & \dots & \dots & \dots \\ 0 & 0 & \dots & 1 \end{bmatrix}$$

However, in [4], the authors show how the approach of two out of n can be cheated. The method of two out of n was extended to k out of n, which works similarly. Instead of having two parts overlaid giving the secret image, it has k parts overlaid giving the secret image [5], [6].

A simple implementation of this scheme proposed in [1], with two shares, is shown in Listing 12-1.

Listing 12-1. Implementation of Shamir's Visual Cryptography Scheme with Two Shares

```
1    clear all;
2    clc;
3    original = imread('apress.JPG');
4    black_white = imbinarize(rgb2gray(original));
5
6    [bw_row0,bw_col0]=size(black_white);
7    share_1=num2cell(ones(bw_row0,bw_col0));
8    share_2=share_1;
9    for i = 1:bw_row0
10       for j = 1:bw_col0
11           if black_white(i,j)==0
```

```
12              rand_pixel = randsrc(1,1,[0 1; 0.5 0.5]);
13                  share_1{i,j}=[rand_pixel ~rand_pixel];
14                  share_2{i,j}=[rand_pixel ~rand_pixel];
15          else
16                  rand_pixel = randsrc(1,1,[0 1; 0.5 0.5]);
17                  share_1{i,j}=[rand_pixel ~rand_pixel];
18                  share_2{i,j}=[~rand_pixel rand_pixel];
19          end
20      end
21  end
22
23  figure;
24  imshow(black_white);
25  title('Black-white image');
26
27  figure;
28  imshow(cell2mat(share_1));
29  title('First Share');
30
31  figure;
32  imshow(cell2mat(share_2));
33  title('Second Share');
34
35  figure;
36  recovered=cell2mat(share_1)+cell2mat(share_2);
37  imshow(recovered);
38  title('Recovered image: Overlapping Share 1 and Share 2');
```

In the code from Listing 12-1, we used the following functions from MATLAB:

- rgb2gray: Converts the colored image taken as input into a grayscale image.

- imbinarize: Converts the grayscale image taken as input in a binarized image, a black and white image (in which only values of 1 and 0 are used for representation).

- `num2cell`: Converts an array into an array of cells, in which each cell contains one element of the initial array.

- `randsrc`: Randomly generates a 1 × 1 matrix from values {0, 1}, where each element has a 0.5 probability of being generated.

- `figure`: Creates a window for the figure.

- `imshow`: Displays the image.

- `cell2mat`: Converts the array of cells into a regular array.

The program works as follows: in Line 3, the image that should be encrypted is read (note that the image should be in the same folder as the source code file) and converted into a grayscale image. Then the grayscale image is converted into a black and white image in Line 4. In Lines 6,7, and 8, the two shares are initialized—these are matrices with the same size as the original image, because, as we have seen, a share is actually an image that has a different transparency than the original secret image.

In Lines 9-20, the two shares are constructed as being permutations of the matrixes C_0, C_1 from above. Then, in Lines 29-38, the four images are displayed (black and white image, share 1, share 2, and the recovered image). The results are shown in Figure 12-1.

The implementation in Listing 12-1 showed a simple example of two shares. In practice, multiple shares are generated and each share is encrypted before being sent on the communication channel; for example, it can be encrypted with AES or RSA cryptosystems. Note that the recovered image—Figure 12-1(e)—is not identical to the original secret image, but it can be deciphered by the human eye.

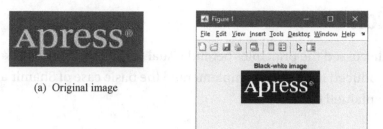

(a) Original image

(b) Black-white image

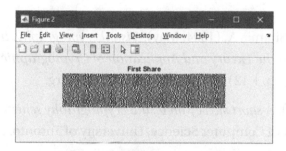

(c) First share

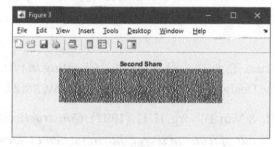

(d) Second share

(e) Recovered image

Figure 12-1. *Images from Shamir's visual cryptography scheme*

Conclusion

This chapter discussed the principles behind visual cryptography and looked at the paper that introduced it. Further, it implemented the basic case of Shamir and Naor's scheme and explained the results.

References

[1]   Naor, M., & Shamir, A. (1994, May). *Visual cryptography. In Workshop on the Theory and Application of Cryptographic Techniques* (pp. 1-12). Springer, Berlin, Heidelberg.

[2]   Cai, J. (2004). *A short survey on visual cryptography schemes.* Department of Computer Science, University of Toronto.

[3]   Zhou, Z., Arce, G. R., & Di Crescenzo, G. (2006). *Halftone visual cryptography.* IEEE transactions on image processing, 15(8), 2441-2453.

[4]   Horng, G., Chen, T., & Tsai, D. S. (2006). *Cheating in visual cryptography.* Designs, Codes and Cryptography, 38(2), 219-236.

[5]   Verheul, E. R., & Van Tilborg, H. C. (1997). *Constructions and properties of k out of n visual secret sharing schemes.* Designs, Codes and Cryptography, 11(2), 179-196.

[6]   Ateniese, G., Blundo, C., De Santis, A., & Stinson, D. R. (2001). *Extended capabilities for visual cryptography.* Theoretical Computer Science, 250(1-2), 143-161.

CHAPTER 13

Chaos-Based Cryptography

Chaos-based cryptography or *chaotic cryptology* is defined as a set of functions (e.g., maps) and other tools (e.g., bifurcation diagram etc.) that apply mathematical chaos theory to the practice of the cryptography. *Chaotic cryptology* has two disciplines— *chaotic cryptography* and *chaotic cryptanalysis.* Chaotic cryptography is the process of encrypting the information and chaotic cryptanalysis is the process of decrypting/ deciphering the encoded/encrypted messages.

Since 1989, when Robert Matthews started researching this unique side of applied cryptography using mathematical chaos theory, the field has been at the peak of theoretical and applied research in cryptography. It has attracted so much interest that chaos-based cryptography now has many applications in different fields, such as health, medical imaging, DNA cryptography, video cryptography, image cryptography, transmissions, telecommunications, and more.

The efficiency of chaos theory in cryptography is based on the implementation of chaotic maps in such a way that the resulting entropy fulfills the *confusion* and *diffusion* properties.

Once we move to the practical side of chaos cryptography, the idea of applying chaos theory and mechanisms in cryptography is very handy and appreciated by a significant number of researchers.

Chaos-based cryptography has encountered various obstacles because it's not quite abstract and other fields must be studied, such as physics and dynamical systems. Despite these obstacles, chaos-based cryptography has been growing significantly since 1990s and is still researched. Every year, significant contributions come about in the literature. Table 13-1 lists some of the most recent and interesting contributions so far.

© Marius Iulian Mihailescu and Stefania Loredana Nita 2021
M. I. Mihailescu and S. L. Nita, *Cryptography and Cryptanalysis in MATLAB*,
https://doi.org/10.1007/978-1-4842-7334-0_13

There is a significant amount of multimedia, graphics, augmented VR applications, etc. Due to this number of applications, authentication is a vulnerable component for any complex system. Research on image authentication is increasing every year and represents a central part of any practical or theoretical system that will be exposed in a real production environment.

Table 13-1. *Similarities and Differences of Chaotic Systems and Cryptography Algorithms According to Reference [15]*

Chaotic Systems	Cryptographic Algorithms
Phase space is a set or subset of real numbers	Phase space is represented by the finite set of integers
Iterations	Rounds
Parameters	Cryptographic key
Change sensitivity to initial conditions and different parameters	Diffusion

Chaos Maps and Functions

Chaos maps or *chaos functions* (depending on the context) are functions that expose chaotic behavior. The maps are characterized by a parameter, which can be discrete or continuous (see a comprehensive list of chaotic maps in reference [19]). Chaos-based cryptography includes discrete maps that use iterated functions.

One point of confusion is the difference between chaos maps and chaos cryptography, where chaos cryptography is defined by finite sets and chaos maps are based on real numbers.

In this chapter, we analyze the logistic map to illustrate chaotic behavior.

Logistic Map

A great, simple instance of a system that behaves chaotically and that can be used in cryptography is the *logistic map*. It was introduced in the demography domain, and it was used as a mathematical model that described the population growth [1]. The logistic map is given by the following expression [2]:

$$x_{n+1} = kx_n\left(1 - x_n\right),$$

where $k \in [0, 4]$ and $x_0 \in (0, 1)$.

The most important element in the expression of the logistic map is the value of k (which is called the *reproduction rate*), because this value dictates the chaotic behavior:

- When $k \in (0, 1)$, the points on the graph of the logistic map's expression approach to 0, independently of the value x_0.

- When $k \in [1, 2)$, the points on the graph of the logistic map's expression approach the value $\frac{k-1}{k}$.

- When $k \in [2, 3)$, the points on the graph of the logistic map's expression also approach the value $\frac{k-1}{k}$, but on an initial phase, they will vary around this value.

- When $k \in [3, 3.44949)$, the points on the graph of the logistic map's expression vary between two values, let's denote them v_1 and v_2. v_1 and v_2 are independent of k.

- When $k \in [3.44949, 3.54409)$, the points on the graph of the logistic map's expression will vary between four values, v_1, v_2, v_3, v_4. When k increases until it has a value of approximately 3.56995, the points on the graph of the logistic map's expression will vary between eight values, then sixteen values, and so on.

- When $k \in (3.5699456, 4]$, the points on the graph are placed chaotically, and it is said that the map is in the chaotic state. The value of n for which the map is stopped is called the dimension of the logistic map.

A more detailed view of these behaviors can be seen in reference [35]. Note that all these values are well-established and computed; see references [32] – [34].

Chaos Theory in Cryptography

As mentioned, dynamic systems play an important role in understanding how different maps work. A chaotic dynamic system is a deterministic system that has a sensitivity to the initial condition. At the same time, the randomness behavior is determined based on the initial condition.

There are several reasons that chaotic systems are suitable for cryptography, such as pseudo-randomness, unpredictability, and sensitivity to initial conditions and parameters.

In reference [15], Ljupco Kocarev presents in a very organized manner all the main concepts that are necessary to begin the journey in the fascinating world of chaos-based cryptography. The article presents the similarities between chaos cryptography and cryptographic algorithms in such a way that it is easy to follow. Also, the author proposes a procedure that can be used as a reference point for designing a chaos-based block encryption algorithm. Based on this procedure and the similarities in Table 13-1, the following discussion is necessary to read before moving to the implementation.

Other tools that are important in order to determine the strength of the algorithm can be summarized as follows:

> *NPCR (Number of Pixel Change Rate)*: An important measure for
> investigating the performance of an image encryption algorithm
> with the goal of testing well the resistance works if a differential
> attack takes place. NPCR shows and computes the change rate of
> pixels and is defined as follows:

$$NPCR = \frac{\sum_{i,j} D(i,j)}{W \times H} \times 100\%$$

> where W and H are the width and height of $ImgC_1$ and $ImgC_2$.
> $ImgC_1$ and $ImgC_2$ are the encryption image versions before/after
> one of the pixels of the image has been changed. $D(i,j)$ is quite
> tricky, especially when it is implemented, and it is has two values
> 1 (if $ImgC_1 \neq ImgC_2$) and 0 (contrary).

Based on this formula, Listing 13-1 shows a basic implementation of NPCR for two images. It is necessary to have two images that are encrypted (see Figure 13-1 for example).

Listing 13-1. NPCR Implementation

```matlab
1   %reading the encrypted images
2   enc_image1=imread('enc_image1.jpg');
3   enc_image2=imread('enc_image2.jpg');
4
5   % compute the size of the of encrypted image
6   % and assigned as rows and columns
7   [rows,columns]=size(enc_image1);
8   step=0;
9   for i=1:1:rows
10      for j=1:1:columns
11          if(enc_image1(i,j)~=enc_image2(i,j))
12              step=step+1;
13          else
14              step=step+0;
15          end
16      end
17  end
18
19  % computing NPCR
20  NPCR =(step/(rows*columns))*100
21
22  % encryption image 1
23  subplot(1,2,1);
24  imshow('enc_image1.jpg');
25  title('Encrypted Image 1');
26
27  % encryption image 2
28  subplot(1,2,2);
29  imshow('enc_image2.jpg');
30  title('Encrypted Image 2');
```

The first step in implementing NPCR is to have two encrypted images, enc_image1 and enc_image2, as shown in Lines 2 and 3. By following the mathematical expression of NPCR and its description, the size is computed in order to set the images' sizes (rows and columns) and iterate through the rows and columns (Lines 9 and 10). Then it computes the 1 and 0 values according to the condition if $ImgC_1 \neq ImgC_2$ (see Lines 11 - 15). In Line 20, we compute the NPCR according to its formula. The result of NPCR on those two images is shown in the Command Window (see Figure 13-1).

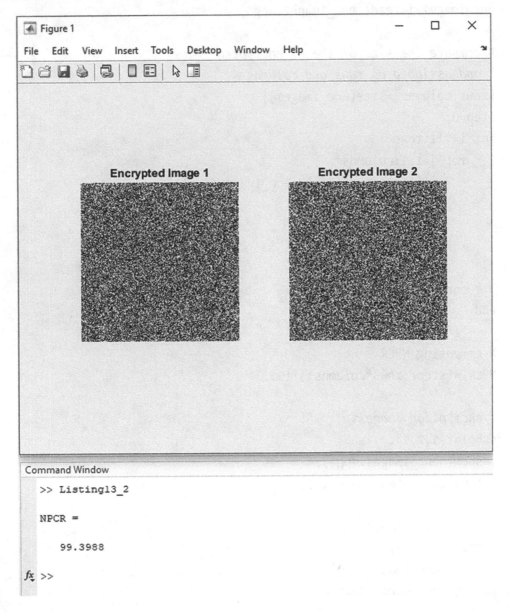

Figure 13-1. NPCR output representation

UACI (Unified Average Changing Intensity): Another important metric. It's the average intensity that characterizes the difference between the plain image and the encrypted image. UACI is defined as follows:

$$UACI = \frac{1}{W \times H} \sum_{i,j} \frac{\left| ImgC_1(i,j) - ImgC_2(i,j) \right|}{255} \times 100\%.$$

Following this expression for UACI, Listing 13-2 shows an elementary implementation. Similar implementations can be seen in multiple sources, such as reference [31]. The same images in Figure 13-1 are used to compute UACI.

Listing 13-2. UACI Implementation

```
1    clear all;
2
3    %load two encrypted images for computing UACI
4    encrypted_image1=imread('enc_image1.jpg');
5    encrypted_image2=imread('enc_image2.jpg');
6
7    %compute the size of the first image
8    [rows,columns]=size(encrypted_image1);
9
10   %create a matrix with rows and columns
11   first_step=zeros(rows,columns);
12
13   %according to the formula presented above
14   for i=1:1:rows
15       for j=1:1:columns
16           if(encrypted_image1(i,j)>encrypted_image2(i,j))
17               first_step(i,j)=(encrypted_image1(i,j)-encrypted_image2(i,j));
18           else
19               first_step(i,j)=(encrypted_image2(i,j)-encrypted_image1(i,j));
20           end
21       end
22   end
23
```

```
24    first_step=first_step/255;
25
26    %computing the next step
27    second_step=0;
28    for i=1:1:rows
29        for j=1:1:columns
30          second_step=second_step+step(i,j);
31        end
32    end
33
34    % the last step is multiplying the result of division between second
      step and
35    % the product of rows with columns, with 100 - according
36    uaci=(second_step/(rows*columns))*100
37
38    % encryption image 1
39    subplot(1,2,1);
40    imshow('enc_image1.jpg');
41    title('Encrypted Image 1');
42
43    % encryption image 2
44    subplot(1,2,2);
45    imshow('enc_image2.jpg');
46    title('Encrypted Image 2');
```

The output of Listing 13-2 is shown in the Command Window and the UACI value for both encrypted images is uaci = 307.4134.

> *Histogram analysis:* The histogram of a specific image is an
> important statistical characteristic that shows the relationship
> between the gray level and its corresponding frequency. If we have
> a very good image encryption algorithm, an encrypted image's
> histogram will have a uniform distribution.

A basic histogram analysis can be performed with the example in Listing 13-3. The output of that histogram analysis is shown Figure 13-2.

Listing 13-3. Implementation of the Histogram Analysis

```
1   %load images
2   encrypted_image_1 = imread('enc_image1.jpg');
3   encrypted_image_2 = imread('enc_image2.jpg');
4
5   % encrypted image 1
6   subplot(1,2,1);
7   imhist(encrypted_image_1);
8   title('Histogram for encrypted image 1');
9
10  % encrypted image 2
11  subplot(1,2,2);
12  imhist(encrypted_image_2);
13  title('Histogram for encrypted image 2');
```

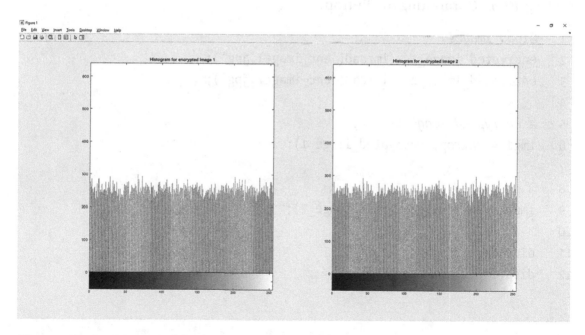

Figure 13-2. Output of the histogram analysis

Entropy Analysis: Once we have an image as input and have applied the encryption process, we need to hide the information in such a way that attackers cannot succeed with their attacks. To be able to provide a proper measurement for uncertainty or complexity of specific images, the authors of reference [30] use two entropy indicators—information entropy and approximate entropy. The entropy $H(x)$ for a specific information source x can be computed as follows:

$$H(x) = -\sum p(x)p(x)$$

where $p(x)$ is defined as the probability of source x.

Entropy is very easy to compute using the entropy function from MATLAB, as shown in Listing 13-4. Figure 13-3 shows the output.

Listing 13-4. Computing the Entropy

```
1    %load images
2    encrypted_image_1 = imread('enc_image1.jpg');
3    encrypted_image_2 = imread('enc_image2.jpg');
4
5    % encrypted image 1
6    img1 = entropy(encrypted_image_1);
7
8    % encrypted image 2
9    img2 = entropy(encrypted_image_2);
10
11   disp(img1);
12   disp(img2);
```

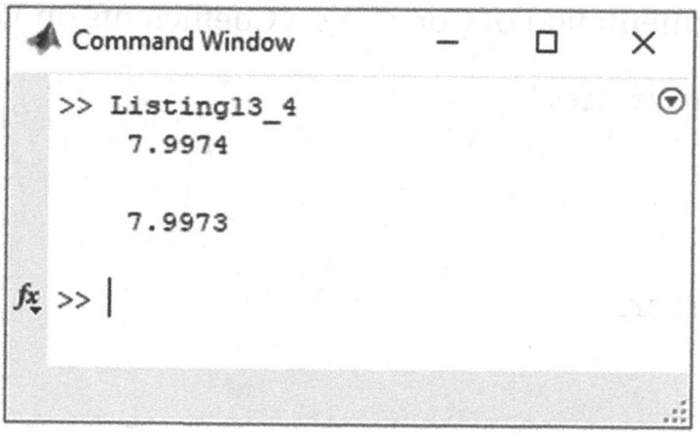

Figure 13-3. *Entropy result*

Key space and sensitivity analysis: Attacks happen every day. The key space size is the most important indicator used to measure the resistance to an attack. To prevent an attack, the key space should be designed to detect somewhere around 2^{128} changes. This should be more than enough to prevent a brute force attack. If we design good image encryption, any change, no matter how small it is, should be sensitive to tiny changes in the cryptographic keys.

Correlation coefficients analysis (CCA): As discussed in previous works, such as references [28] and [29], correlation analysis is a very useful tool that measures the success rate of an attack on the encrypted image. The correlation is applied between adjacent pixels that are characterized with correlation coefficients. CCA is defined as follows:

$$r_{var_x, var_y} = \frac{C(var_x, var_y)}{\sqrt{D(var_x) \cdot D(var_y)}}$$

where var_x and var_y represent the grayscale value of two pixels from the image given as input. $D(var_x)$ and $D(var_y)$ represent the variances of x and y. $C(var_x, var_y)$ represent the covariance for x and y.

The correlation coefficients can run on different aspects, such as x-axis, y-axis, rows, columns, etc. For this work, we choose to show how to corelate the coefficients on vertical (see Listing 13-5 and Figure 13-4).

Listing 13-5. Implementation of Correlation Coefficients on Vertical

```
1    %correlation on vertical
2    clc;
3    clear all;
4
5    %control parameters
6    ctrl_p_1=0;
7    ctrl_p_2=0;
8    indexJ = 1;
9    indexI = 1;
10
11   %load the image for which the correlation should be performed
12   encrypted_image=imread('enc_image1.jpg');
13
14   %use the encrypted image and represented it as a RGB version and not as a
15   %grayscale version conversion
16   representation_as_rgb=encrypted_image;
17
18   %computing the size in order to represented as a matrix of rows and
     columns
19   [rows,columns]=size(representation_as_rgb);
20
21   %compute the total length by multiplying rows with columns
22   total_length=rows*columns;
23
24   %generate structure with zeroes from 1 to 10240 (256*40)
25   x_axis=zeros(1,(256*40));
26   y_axis=zeros(1,(256*40));
27
28   while indexJ <= 80
29       while indexI <= rows
30           if(mod(indexJ,2)==0)
31               ctrl_p_1=ctrl_p_1+1;
32               x_axis(1,ctrl_p_1)=representation_as_rgb(indexI,indexJ);
```

```
33              indexI = indexI+1;
34              indexJ = indexJ+1;
35              disp(x_axis(1,ctrl_p_1));
36         else
37              ctrl_p_2=ctrl_p_2+1;
38              y_axis(1,ctrl_p_2)=representation_as_rgb(indexI,indexJ);
39              indexI = indexI+1;
40              indexJ = indexJ+1;
41              disp(y_axis(1,ctrl_p_2));
42         end
43     end
44  end
45
46  %figure
47  scatter(x_axis,y_axis,2)
48  title('Encrypted image 1 - Enc(Img1) - vertical correlation');
49  ENC_IMG1 = corrcoef(x_axis,y_axis)
```

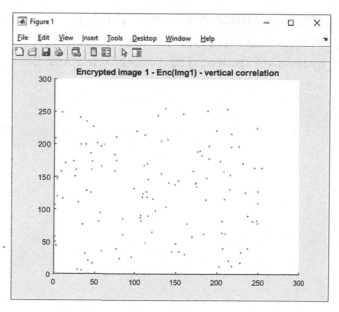

Figure 13-4. *Correlation coefficients on vertical*

Sensitivity to Initial Conditions

Sensitivity to initial conditions is one of the most important requirements of dynamic systems. The goal is to ensure chaotic behavior based on sensitivity to the initial conditions. When the iteration process, based on an initial set of values, takes place on a dynamic system, the result is represented by a trajectory. Once small changes are made to the same set of initial values, the trajectory is different from the first set of values.

In practice, the *Lyapunov Exponent* determines the sensitivity to the initial condition. The tool shows the divergence criteria of the trajectories that serve the initial values.

The Lyapunov Exponent is mathematically expressed as: $|az(t)| \approx e\lambda|\alpha Zo|$, where λ is the Lyapunov Exponent. For more details about how to use it in MATLAB, see reference [27]. It includes a very good example of how the Lyapunov Exponent can be applied in practice using MATLAB, where `lorenzAttractorExampleData.mat` is the sample data set and the computation process is done with the data from the x-axis. This example is shown in Listing 13-6 and the output is shown in Figure 13-5.

Listing 13-6. Computing the Lyapunov Exponent [27]

```
load('lorenzAttractorExampleData.mat','data','fs');
plot3(data(:,1),data(:,2),data(:,3));
title('Computing Lyapunov Exponent for Lorenz Attractor Data Set');
```

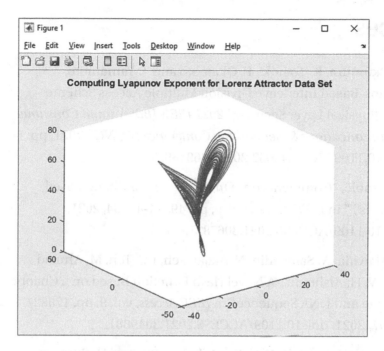

Figure 13-5. Computation of the Lyapunov Exponent

Conclusion

This chapter discussed chaos-based cryptography in depth. It covered its tools/mechanisms and explained how it can be used in practice.

By the end of this chapter, you should:

- Have a comprehensive image of what chaos-based cryptography's main purpose is and understand the main tools and maps used in practice in order to encrypt/decrypt the images.

- Have a useful journey through the main tools used to determine security and detect how sensitive is. These tools are represented by NPCR, UACI, histogram analysis, entropy analysis, key space and sensitivity analysis, and correlation coefficients analysis.

References

[1]   M. Okumura, K. Tomoki, E. Okamoto and T. Yamamoto, "Chaos-Based Interleave Division Multiple Access Scheme with Physical Layer Security," *2021 IEEE 18th Annual Consumer Communications & Networking Conference (CCNC)*, 2021, pp. 1-2, doi: 10.1109/CCNC49032.2021.9369489.

[2]   D. Lambić, "Comments on "On the Design of Chaos-Based S-Boxes", " in *IEEE Access*, vol. 9, pp. 49354-49354, 2021, doi: 10.1109/ACCESS.2021.3067821.

[3]   M. Alawida, A. Samsudin, N. Alajarmeh, J. S. Teh, M. Ahmad and W. H. Alshoura, "A Novel Hash Function Based on a Chaotic Sponge and DNA Sequence," in *IEEE Access*, vol. 9, pp. 17882-17897, 2021, doi: 10.1109/ACCESS.2021.3049881.

[4]   L. Moysis, I. Kafetzis, C. Volos, A. V. Tutueva and D. Butusov, "Application of a Hyperbolic Tangent Chaotic Map to Random Bit Generation and Image Encryption," *2021 IEEE Conference of Russian Young Researchers in Electrical and Electronic Engineering (ElConRus)*, 2021, pp. 559-565, doi: 10.1109/ElConRus51938.2021.9396395.

[5]   M. S. Hasan, P. S. Paul, M. Sadia and M. R. Hossain, "Integrated Circuit Design of an Improved Discrete Chaotic Map by Averaging Multiple Seed Maps," *SoutheastCon 2021*, 2021, pp. 1-6, doi: 10.1109/SoutheastCon45413.2021.9401848.

[6]   T. M. Hoang, "Perturbed Chaotic Map with Varying Number of Iterations and Application in Image Encryption," *2020 IEEE Eighth International Conference on Communications and Electronics (ICCE)*, 2021, pp. 413-418, doi: 10.1109/ICCE48956.2021.9352070.

[7]   Je Sen Teh, Moatsum Alawida, You Cheng Sii, "Implementation and practical problems of chaos-based cryptography revisited," *Journal of Information Security and Applications,* Volume 50, 2020, 102421, ISSN 2214-2126. DOI: https://doi.org/10.1016/j.jisa.2019.102421.

[8]   P. T. Akkasaligar and S. Biradar, "Medical Image Compression and
       Encryption using Chaos based DNA Cryptography," *2020 IEEE
       Bangalore Humanitarian Technology Conference (B-HTC)*, 2020,
       pp. 1-5, doi: 10.1109/B-HTC50970.2020.9297928.

[9]   W. A. Nassan, T. Bonny and A. Baba, "A New Chaos-Based
       Cryptosystem for Voice Encryption," *2020 3rd International
       Conference on Signal Processing and Information Security
       (ICSPIS)*, 2020, pp. 1-4, doi: 10.1109/ICSPIS51252.2020.9340132.

[10]   S. Ergün, "Estimating Secret Parameter and Vulnerability Analysis
       of a Chaos-Based RNG," *IEEE EUROCON 2019 -18th International
       Conference on Smart Technologies*, 2019, pp. 1-4, doi: 10.1109/
       EUROCON.2019.8861998.

[11]   A. A. Zaher and G. Amjad Hussain, "Chaos-based Cryptography
       for Transmitting Multimedia Data over Public Channels,"
       *2019 7th International Conference on Information and
       Communication Technology (ICoICT)*, 2019, pp. 1-6, doi: 10.1109/
       ICoICT.2019.8835351.

[12]   A. A. Zaher and J. Yousafzai, "An Adaptive Control Approach
       to Securely Transmit Colored Images using Chaos-based
       Cryptography," *2019 IEEE 62nd International Midwest Symposium
       on Circuits and Systems (MWSCAS)*, 2019, pp. 953-956, doi:
       10.1109/MWSCAS.2019.8885161.

[13]   M. Sharma and A. Sharma, "A secret file sharing scheme
       with chaos based encryption," *2019 10th International
       Conference on Computing, Communication and Networking
       Technologies (ICCCNT)*, 2019, pp. 1-7, doi: 10.1109/
       ICCCNT45670.2019.8944344.

[14]   J. Ahmad, A. Tahir, J. S. Khan, A. Jameel, Q. H. Abbasi and
       W. Buchanan, "A Novel Multi-Chaos Based Compressive Sensing
       Encryption Technique," *2019 International Conference on
       Advances in the Emerging Computing Technologies (AECT)*, 2020,
       pp. 1-4, doi: 10.1109/AECT47998.2020.9194220.

[15]   Kocarev, L., editor. *Chaos-Based Cryptography*. Springer, 2011.

[16] D. Curiac, D. Iercan, O. Dranga, F. Dragan and O. Banias, "Chaos-Based Cryptography: End of the Road?," *The International Conference on Emerging Security Information, Systems, and Technologies (SECUREWARE 2007)*, 2007, pp. 71-76, doi: 10.1109/ SECUREWARE.2007.4385313.

[17] Mishkovski I., Kocarev L. (2011) Chaos-Based Public-Key Cryptography. In: Kocarev L., Lian S. (eds) *Chaos-Based Cryptography. Studies in Computational Intelligence,* vol 354. Springer, Berlin, Heidelberg. https://doi.org/10.1007/978-3- 642-20542-2_2.

[18] L. Kocarev, "Chaos-based cryptography: a brief overview," in *IEEE Circuits and Systems Magazine*, vol. 1, no. 3, pp. 6-21, 2001, doi: 10.1109/7384.963463.

[19] List of chaotic maps. Available online: https://en.wikipedia. org/wiki/List_of_chaotic_maps

[20] Marius Iulian Mihailescu, "New Enrollment Scheme for Biometric Template Using Hash Chaos-based Cryptography," *Procedia Engineering*, Volume 69, 2014, Pages 1459-1468, ISSN 1877-7058. DOI: https://doi.org/10.1016/j.proeng.2014.03.142.

[21] Nita, Stefania L.; Mihailescu, Marius I.; Pau, Valentin C. 2018. "Security and Cryptographic Challenges for Authentication Based on Biometrics Data" *Cryptography* 2, no. 4: 39. https://doi. org/10.3390/cryptography2040039

[22] Dăscălescu, A.C., Boriga, R.E. "A novel fast chaos-based algorithm for generating random permutations with high shift factor suitable for image scrambling." *Nonlinear Dyn* **74,** 307–318 (2013). https://doi.org/10.1007/s11071-013-0969-6.

[23] Ana-Cristina Dăscălescu, Radu Eugen Boriga, Adrian-Viorel Diaconu, "Study of a New Chaotic Dynamical System and Its Usage in a Novel Pseudorandom Bit Generator", *Mathematical Problems in Engineering*, vol. 2013, Article ID 769108, 10 pages, 2013. https://doi.org/10.1155/2013/769108

[24]   Boriga, R.; Dăscălescu, A.C.; Diaconu, A.V. "A New One-Dimensional Chaotic Map and its Use in a Novel Real Time Image Encryption Scheme." *Adv. Multimed* 2014, 2014.

[25]   Boriga, R.; Dăscălescu, A.C.; Diaconu, A.V. "A New Fast Image Encryption Scheme Based on 2D Chaotic Maps." *IAENG Int. J. Comput. Sci* 2014, 41, 249–258.

[26]   Dăscălescu, A.C.; Boriga, R.; Mihăilescu, M.I. "A Novel Chaos-Based Image Encryption Scheme.: *Ann. Univ. Craiova Math. Comput. Sci. Ser* 2014, 41, 47–58.

[27]   Lyapunov Exponent. Available online: https://www.mathworks.com/help/predmaint/ref/lyapunovexponent.html

[28]   Mihailescu, Marius Iulian, and Stefania Loredana Nita. *Pro Cryptography and Cryptanalysis: Creating Advanced Algorithms with C# and .NET.* Apress, 2021. DOI: 10.1007/978-1-4842-6367-9.

[29]   Mihailescu, Marius Iulian, and Stefania Loredana Nita. *Pro Cryptography and Cryptanalysis with C++20: Creating and Programming Advanced Algorithms.* Apress, 2021. DOI: 10.1007/978-1-4842-6586-4.

[30]   S. M. Pincus, "Approximate entropy as a measure of system complexity," Proceedings of the National Academy of Sciences, vol. 88, no. 6, pp. 2297–2301, 1991.

[31]   A New Approach of Image Encryption using 3D. Available online: https://github.com/billalkuet07/A-New-Approach-of-Image-Encryption-Using-3D.

[32]   May, R. M. (2004). "Simple mathematical models with very complicated dynamics." *The Theory of Chaotic Attractors,* 85-93.

[33]   Devaney, R. (2018). *An introduction to chaotic dynamical systems.* CRC Press. ISBN-13: 978-0-8133-4085.

[34]   Liu, W., Sun, K., & Zhu, C. (2016). *A fast image encryption algorithm based on chaotic map. Optics and Lasers in Engineering,* 84, 26-36.

[35]   Logistic Map. Available online: `https://en.wikipedia.org/` `wiki/Logistic_map#Special_cases_of_the_map`.

CHAPTER 14

Steganography

The goal of this chapter is to describe the main algorithms and methods used in steganography and explain how they can be implemented in MATLAB.

Before providing a definition of *steganography*, it is important to explain that steganography uses different media to hide messages, including images, text files, video files, and sound files. Based on the media in which the information is hidden, different definitions have been proposed. Most of the research and practical implementations have been for image, text, and video files. Different authors have proposed different definitions of steganography, adjusting the definitions based on the requirements and purposes of their research. That being said, the main definition of *steganography* is that it represents the art of hiding data within a media file (sound, image, or video) or text file.

The process of hiding information involves the general step of selecting the media file (e.g., the image file) or text file, which then leads to two image files. One is called the cover-image and the second one, which is obtained after applying the steganography algorithm/method, is called the *stego-image.*

When we use image files to hide information, the image is represented in two ways, as a matrix that is being stored in memory. For example: (1) $a \times b$ matrix for grayscale images and (2) $a \times b \times 3$ matrix for color images. Each item in the matrix is represented by a value that shows the intensity of a pixel. The message is embedded in the image by modifying the values of random pixels. The random pixels are chosen by the encryption algorithm/method. In this situation, the user who receives the *stego-image* has to be aware of the algorithm used in the encryption process.

© Marius Iulian Mihailescu and Stefania Loredana Nita 2021
M. I. Mihailescu and S. L. Nita, *Cryptography and Cryptanalysis in MATLAB,*
https://doi.org/10.1007/978-1-4842-7334-0_14

Algorithms and Methods for Different Steganography Types

Steganography for Image Files

Algorithms used in steganography for images can be summarized as follows:

- *Least significant bit (LSB) insertion*: One of the most important algorithms for image steganography. This algorithm is based on a process that modifies the LSB level of a specific image. The message is encoded and stored among the LSB in the pixels. In some literature reviews, the pixels that hold the hidden information are considered random noise.

- *Filtering and masking:* These techniques are dedicated to 24-bit grayscale images. The information is hidden as watermarks on physical paper. In some cases, they are digital watermarks.

- *Encryption and scattering:* The message is hidden as white noise and is more secure than the LSB method.

Steganography for Audio Files

Hiding secret messages in audio files is one of the most challenging techniques in steganography. The following list includes some of the best known techniques:

- *Spread spectrum:* The secret message is spread out as much as possible across the audio signal frequency.

- *LSB encoding:* LSB encoding has a very interesting behavior when it is used to encode/hide secret messages in audio, due to the fact that it does not create consistent changes to the sound.

- *Parity coding:* The signal is divided into separate areas or regions, known as *samples*. The secret message is encoded in each bit from the hidden information in a parity bit from a sample area.

- *Echo hiding:* The process of echo hiding embeds the sound file by adding an echo to a separated signal.

- *Phase coding:* The method uses the fact that the components specific to a sound phase are not audible to the human ear.

Steganography for Video Files

When using video files, an extra amount of data is used to hide the secret data. The most commonly known approaches in steganography for video are:

- *Insertion using least significant bit:* The method treats the video file as separated frames. The changes are applied to the display image in each frame.

- *Real-time video steganography:* The hidden information is on the image that is served as the output on a specific or dedicated device.

Practical Implementation

Implementing the Least Significant Bit (LSB) Method

Listing 14-1 provides a simple, basic implementation of hiding information (text) in an image using the least significant bit (LSB) method. A similar solution can be seen in [1] and [10], without the optimization steps.

Listing 14-1. Hiding Information (Text) Using LSB

```
1   % variables
2   binary_representation = '';
3   image = '';
4   hidden_image = '';
5   rValues = '';
6   cValues = '';
7   ccValues = '';
8   string_length = '';
9   ascii_representation = '';
10  ascii_binary_representation = '';
11  control_bit=''; % used to count how many bits were hidden
12
13  % read the image used for hidden process,
14  % convert it to the grayscale if the image is RGB
15  image=imread(swan.jpg');
16
```

```
17    % compute the size of the image and store the
18    % values for rows, columns and color of channels
19    % rValues - rows number/value
20    % cValues - columns number/value
21    % ccValues - number of the color channels
22    [rValues, cValues, ccValues] = size(image);
23
24    % provide the conversion from color to grayscale if the color
      channels
25    % number is bigger and strict with 1
26    if ccValues > 1
27        image = rgb2gray(image);
28    end
29
30    % initialize the image that will be used for hiding with the image
      obtained
31    % due to the conversion process from color to grayscale.
32    hidden_image=image;
33
34    % read the message that will be hide within the images
35    hidden_message=input('Provide a message that will be hidden in
      the image: ','s');
36
37    % very important step is to understand that each character from the
38    % message entered by the user is represented as 1 byte = 8 bits.
39    % we will require to compute the length of the entire message by
      multiplying
40    % it's length with 8 (bits).
41    string_length=strlength(hidden_message)*8;
42
43    % compute the ascii values by computing unsigned integer values with
      only 8
44    % bits of information for the hidden message entered above.
45    ascii_representation=uint8(hidden_message);
46
```

```
47   % convert the decimal to binary the ascii values with only 8 bits of
48   % information and store them in
49   ascii_binary_representation=dec2bin(ascii_representation,8);
50
51   % store the binary values of ascii value as a string
52   for i=1:strlength(hidden_message)
53       binary_representation=append(binary_representation,ascii_binary_
         representation(i,:));
54   end
55
56   for i=1:rValues              % row index
57       for j=1:cValues          % column index
58           control_bit=1;
59           if control_bit<=string_length
60               % compute using modulo 2 the grey level for each of the
                 pixel
61               modulo = mod(image(i,j),2);
62               least_significant_bit=modulo;
63
64               %Convert the bit from the message to numeric form
65
66               % compute the binary representation of the bit that
                 represents
67               % the numeric form
68               binaryRepresentation = binary_representation(control_bit);
69
70               % convert string to double for the binary representation
71               doubleBinaryRepresentation=str2double(binaryRepresentation);
72
73               % compute the XOR for the bit and least significant bit
74               xor_temp = xor(least_significant_bit,doubleBinary
                 Representation);
75               xor_temp_to_double = double(xor_temp);
76
```

```
77              % Change the bit of the image_hide accordingly
78              % compute the addition between the pixel and xor
                double value
79              addition_pixel_xor = image(i,j)+xor_temp_to_double;
80
81              % add the addition result to a specific
82              % pixel from the hidden image
83              hidden_image(i,j) = addition_pixel_xor;
84
85              % move to the next bit
86              control_bit=control_bit+1;
87          end
88      end
89   end
90
91   % original image representation
92   subplot(1,2,1);
93   imshow(image);
94   title('Original image');
95
96   % new image with the message hidden
97   subplot(1,2,2);
98   imshow(hidden_image);
99   title('Hidden image');
100
101  sgt = sgtitle('Hiding information to image using LSB
     method','Color','blue');
102  sgt.FontSize = 20;
103  imwrite(hidden_image,'swan_output.png');
```

This solution is optimized in such a way that the time execution is faster compared to other exhaustive solutions that don't provide optimization features.

For this example, we choose a personal image. This is a standard image that can be used in most fields of steganography (see Figure 14-1a). Figure 14-1b shows the grayscale version of the original image. The grayscale image is computed in Line 27 of Listing 14-1.

Figure 14-1a. *Lena image [9] used for the LSB method (see Line 15 of Listing 14-1)*

Figure 14-1b. *The output: the grayscale version of the original image*

We enter a hidden message as an example (`welcometoapress`) and this output is shown in Figures 14-2 and 14-3.

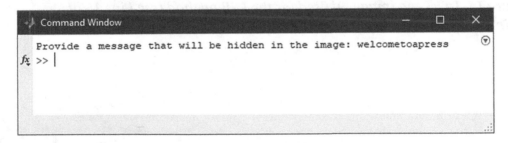

Figure 14-2. *Providing the message that will be hidden*

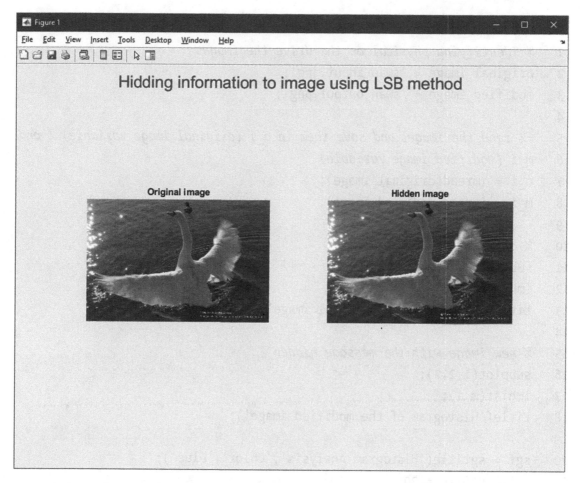

Figure 14-3.   Representation of the output

Implementing the Histogram Analysis Method

Histogram analysis is one of the most important methods used to analyze images and detect if an image has been modified or not. In order to determine if an image has been modified, it's important to be able to compute a histogram analysis on the original image (without any information hidden in it). The next step is to compare the histogram analyses of the two images (the modified image and the original).

Listing 14-2 shows how a histogram analysis can be implemented for two images (an original image and a modified image that contains hidden information).

Listing 14-2. Implementing the Histogram Analysis Method

```
1    % Identifying physical on the drive the images
2    original_image = 'swan_input.jpg';
3    modified_image = 'swan_output.png';
4
5     % read the images and save them in o_i (original image variable) % and
6    m_i (modified image variable)
7    o_i = imread(original_image);
8    m_i = imread(modified_image);
9
10   % original image
11   subplot(1,2,1);
12   imhist(o_i);
13   title('Histogram for original image');
14
15   % new image with the message hidden
16   subplot(1,2,2);
17   imhist(m_i);
18   title('Histogram of the modified image');
19
20   sgt = sgtitle('Histogram Analysis','Color','blue');
21   sgt.FontSize = 20;
```

Once the example in Listing 14-2 is executed, both histograms are represented and shown, as in Figure 14-4. You can easily observe the differences between the original image (left) and the image that contains the hidden information (right).

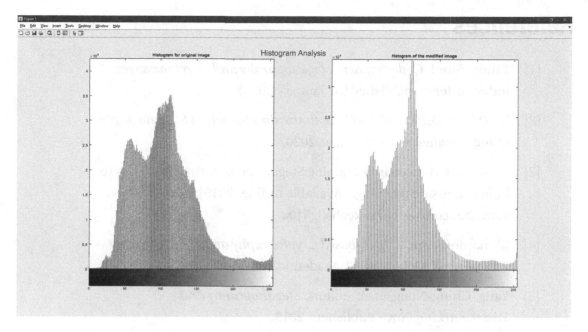

Figure 14-4. *Histogram analysis of both images, the original (left) and the hidden image (right)*

Conclusion

This chapter discussed the most important components of hiding information in different media files. It examined some basic implementations and reviewed the main steps necessary for such implementations.

Steganography/steganalysis is a complex field. To provide a comprehensive study (theoretical and practical) would require a book to itself. Researchers from all over the world are publishing significant information about steganography and steganalysis every year.

The practical implementations provided in this chapter should help you begin to see how steganography and steganalysis algorithms are designed, adjusted for real and independent scenarios, and implemented.

References

[1]   Tanna, Sunil. *Codes, ciphers, steganography and secret messages.* Independently published (31 January 2020).

[2]   SARMAH, DIPTI KAPOOR. *Optimization Models in Steganography Using Metaheuristics.* Springer, 2020.

[3]   Edureka. Cybersecurity Training Steganography Tutorial – How to hide text inside the image. Available online (2019): `https://www.youtube.com/watch?v=xepNoHgNjOw`

[4]   Mohamed, Amr. *A DNA-based Cryptography and Steganography Technique.* LAP LAMBERT Academic Publishing, 2017.

[5]   Yang, Ching-Nung, et al., editors. *Steganography and Watermarking.* Nova Publishers, 2013.

[6]   Schaathun, Hans Georg. *Machine Learning in Image Steganalysis.* IEEE/Wiley, 2012.

[7]   Böhme, Rainer. *Advanced Statistical Steganalysis.* Springer-Verlag, 2010.

[8]   Steganography Algorithm. Available online: `http://matlab.algorithmexamples.com/web/algorithms/ImageProcessing/LSB%20based%20Image%20Steganography/steganography.html`.

[9]   Lenna or Lena. Available online: `https://en.wikipedia.org/wiki/Lenna`.

[10] Steganography Algorithm. Available online: `https://www.geeksforgeeks.org/lsb-based-image-steganography-using-matlab/`.

Index

© Marius Iulian Mihailescu and Stefania Loredana Nita 2021
M. I. Mihailescu and S. L. Nita, *Cryptography and Cryptanalysis in MATLAB*,
https://doi.org/10.1007/978-1-4842-7334-0